BOOKS for you to make

Also by Susan Purdy

CHRISTMAS DECORATIONS FOR YOU TO MAKE

COSTUMES FOR YOU TO MAKE

FESTIVALS FOR YOU TO CELEBRATE

HOLIDAY CARDS FOR YOU TO MAKE

IF YOU HAVE A YELLOW LION

JEWISH HOLIDAYS

MY LITTLE CABBAGE

BOOKS
for you to make

Written and Illustrated

by

SUSAN PURDY

J.B. LIPPINCOTT COMPANY

PHILADELPHIA AND NEW YORK

Copyright © 1973 by Susan Purdy
All rights reserved
Printed in the United States of America
Second Printing

The author acknowledges permission to reproduce photographs from the following sources: Elmer C. Hill, Jr., Kingsport Press, pages 82, 89, 90, 91, 92; C. Robert Erdman, Rae Publishing Company, top of page 84. All other photographs used in this book were taken by the author at Rae Publishing Co., Inc., Cedar Grove, New Jersey.

U. S. Library of Congress Cataloging in Publication Data

Purdy, Susan Gold, birth date
  Books for you to make.

  SUMMARY: Step-by-step instructions for making up and binding a book. Includes several binding techniques.
1. Books—Juvenile literature. [1. Books. 2. Bookbinding] I. Title.
Z4.Z9P87   686   73-4568
ISBN-0-397-31318-7 (reinforced bdg.)

*For his constant encouragement, this
is affectionately dedicated to
Ken W. Purdy
who loved a skillfully-turned phrase
and a well-written book.*

Acknowledgments

Many people have contributed to the inspiration for this book. I would particularly like to thank Marjorie Hansen and her children's literature classes at the University of Bridgeport; the children and faculties of the Wilton, Connecticut, schools including especially Mrs. Barbara Redd and Mrs. Grace Dazé; Jeanne Vestal, and my sister Nancy Gold Lieberman. For their help in the preparation of this manuscript I wish to thank Tere LoPrete, Ellen Kagan, Ed Bathmann of Rae Publishing Co., Inc., Kenneth L. Dockery and Elmer C. Hill, Jr. of Kingsport Press, Joan Sommer, Gus Merwin, and Rachel and Stephan Chodorov. For Everything, including proofreading galleys and checking drawings, I thank, with love, my husband Geoffrey Purdy.

CONTENTS

I. WRITE YOUR OWN BOOK! 11
   A. Why Write a Book? 11
   B. What Should You Write About? 12
   C. How Do You Begin? 12
   D. How Do You Revise the Manuscript? 13
   E. How Do You Turn the Manuscript into a Book? 13

II. A SPECIAL BOOKBINDER'S VOCABULARY 14

III. WHAT WILL YOUR BOOK LOOK LIKE?
DUMMY, DESIGN, LAYOUT, AND ILLUSTRATIONS 15
   A. How Do You Design a Book? 15
   B. How Do You Make A Dummy? 16
   C. How Do You Lay Out Pages? 17
   D. How Is the Text Placed in the Bound Book? 18
   E. Should You Number the Pages of Your Book? 19
   F. How Do You Plan the Illustrations? 19
   G. What Technique Should You Use for the Illustrations? 20
   H. How Do You Actually Illustrate? 21

IV. WHAT KIND OF BINDING SHOULD YOU USE? 22

V. MATERIALS LIST 24

VI. BASIC SKILLS 26

   A. How to Cut a Straight Edge on Paper or Cardboard 26
   B. How to Cut Fabric "on the Grain" 26
   C. How to Fold Paper "on the Grain" 27
   D. How to Strengthen Cotton Sewing Thread 27
   E. Hole-Measuring Guides for Sewn Bindings 28
      1. 3-Hole Guide 28
      2. 5-Hole Guide 29
   F. Sewing Methods 30
      1. 3-Hole Sewing Method 30
      2. 5-Hole Sewing Method 31

VII.	SIMPLE BINDINGS	32
	A. Stapled Binding	32
	B. Brass Fastener Binding	34
	C. Sewn Binding	35
VIII.	OTHER BINDINGS	36
	A. Single Sheets Sewn to Hinged Boards	36
	B. Folding and Sewing a Single Signature	45
	C. Single-Signature Book, Half-Bound	48
	D. Multi-Signature Book, Full-Bound with Case	57
IX.	THE DUST JACKET	68
	A. Purposes	68
	B. How to Make It	69
X.	LET'S LOOK AT A PRINTED BOOK	72
	A. What Does It Look Like?	72
	B. What Can You Learn from the Pages?	72
XI.	HOW ARE PRINTED BOOKS MADE?	76
	A. What Is the First Step?	76
	B. How Does a Book Get Published?	76
	C. What Exactly Does the Publisher Do?	77
	D. What Does the Printer Do?	78
	E. How Are Books Printed?	80
	F. How Is Artwork Printed?	86
	G. How Are Printed Sheets Turned into Bound Books?	89
	H. How Long Does It Take to Make a Book?	93
INDEX		94

I. WRITE YOUR OWN BOOK!

A. Why Write a Book?

Books are written and printed so that ideas can be kept a long time, protected, and easily shared with people. There are many other ways to communicate ideas: for example talking, dancing, acting, or playing a musical instrument. These forms, however, must be recreated each time they are shared, while others, such as films, recorded tapes, or paintings, are like books, and can be kept as they are and shared many times over.

When you handwrite and hand-bind your own book you will be joining a long and ancient tradition. More than two thousand years ago in Mesopotamia and Asia Minor, writers called *scribes* wrote by scratching letters into tablets of clay with a sharp tool called a *stylus*. Writing was so important to civilization even at that time that some of these tablets were kept in royal libraries.

The early Egyptian scribes wrote with reed pens and colored inks in rolls (some one hundred feet long) of papyrus "paper." These rolls are called *scrolls*. The Greeks and Romans also used papyrus scrolls, as well as waxed wooden tablets. At least three thousand years ago the Chinese were making handwritten books on wood or bamboo strips, and by the second century A.D. they had invented the first wood-pulp paper, the kind we use today, though it did not reach the Western world until about one thousand years later. The early Hebrews wrote on parchment made of dried, scraped, stretched animal skins.

Parchment was also used in Europe during the Middle Ages, when books were made in monasteries and written by monks who were also scribes. They made some scrolls, but worked mainly on books bound at the side called *codices*. Bookbinding as we know it originated with the need to fasten a side-bound *codex* together. Some of the most beautiful bookbinding in the world was done for the Church during the Middle Ages, when gold, silver, rare leathers, and precious jewels were used to make book covers.

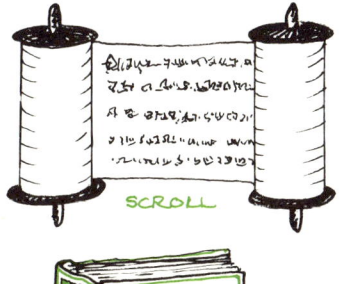

By the fifteenth century in the West, paper commonly took the place of parchment. Movable type had been invented in Holland, and perfected in Germany by Johann Gutenberg, and because printing was faster, cheaper, and more reliable, printed books generally replaced handwritten ones. As a craft, however, books such as yours are still made by hand.

B. What Should You Write About?

All you need to get started is an idea you want to share or preserve. Everyone has ideas. You can write about your dreams, hopes, fantasies . . . go for a long quiet walk with your imagination. If you make up stories and write them down, you will be writing *fiction*. You may prefer, on the other hand, to write about things you have actually seen rather than things you have imagined. This kind of writing is called *nonfiction*. This book is nonfiction, as are books about science, history, travel, crafts, and real people. Fairy tales, on the other hand, belong in the fiction category. If you write in sentences, in the manner of ordinary speech, you are writing *prose*. If you write in verse, it is called *poetry*.

C. How Do You Begin?

Simply pick up a pencil and a piece of paper and get started. Or, you might prefer to type, or talk into a tape recorder. Authors differ in the way they work. Each author must find the way that is best for him.

When you are ready to begin, tell your whole story at once in a rough *first draft*, a sort of working skeleton which you will add to and fill out later. Don't worry about spelling or grammar. Don't worry about what to say first. You can correct and organize your material in the next step. Concentrate on ideas now. Write simply and directly. Let your writing have its own personality. Write freely and happily because you have something you want to say. Do not be afraid that it has to be perfect just because it is written down. Write until you are finished. Your book can be as long or as short as you wish, for YOU are the author.

D. How Do You Revise the Manuscript?

After you finish the first draft, reread it. It may help you to read it aloud to yourself or to a friend so you can hear the sound of your own sentences. Are they clear and expressive? Are they long and confused? It is not easy to criticize your own work, but this is an essential part of being an author.

Consider the organization of the material in your first draft. Does each part come in its logical place? Should some sentences or sections be switched around to make things clearer? Now you can think about grammar, punctuation, paragraphs, and chapter divisions. You will probably wish to write a second draft to include changes. The last, or final, draft is the *completed manuscript*.

E. How Do You Turn the Manuscript into a Book?

After you are finished writing and revising, you will want to decide what the manuscript will look like in book form. Using the directions that follow, you can decide on the shape, size, and method of fastening, or binding, as well as the type of illustrations you will use. Then you will make a working model, or *dummy*, of the book's pages so you can decide how the text and illustrations will be arranged. The pages are then gathered and fastened together, and paper or cardboard covers are attached by various methods.

II. A SPECIAL BOOKBINDER'S VOCABULARY

Like all craftsmen, bookbinders have their own special vocabulary. A few of their terms, used in this book, are italicized below.

The top edge of a book is called the *head*, the bottom edge the *foot*, the open side the *fore-edge*, and the fastened side the *spine*.

A group of folded and sewn pages is called a *signature*. The same term is used for the large, professionally printed sheet of paper which is machine-folded into many pages. A working model of a book is called a *dummy*.

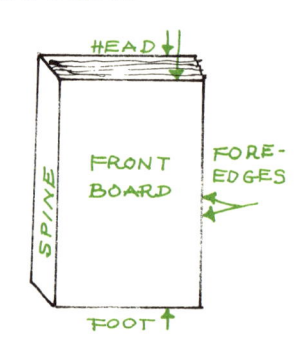

When front and back covers are made of stiff material, they are called *boards*. Paper or other material glued over the boards is *cover paper*; material covering the spine is the *spine cover*. When the cover consists of stiff front, back, and spine boards, it is called a *case*; when the book is attached to the case it is said to be *cased-in*.

The pages that are glued flat onto the front and back boards to secure the binding are called *endpapers*. The loose page next to each endpaper is the *flyleaf*. A removable paper cover is called a *dust jacket*.

There are many different types of binding as you will see in Chapter IV. Among the basic styles described in this book are:

Quarter-Bound: Cloth or tape covers the spine, and the front and back boards are made of cardboard covered with decorative material.

Half-Bound: Like the quarter-bound, except that the material covering the spine also covers the corners of the front and back boards.

Full-Bound: The front, back, and spine are all made of cardboard covered with decorative material.

III. WHAT WILL YOUR BOOK LOOK LIKE?
Dummy, Design, Layout, and Illustrations

You are the designer and illustrator as well as the author of your book. You can make it look any way you choose. When planning, however, remember that a book must be both attractive *and* easy to read. Your book's overall design, as well as the style of illustration, should be related to the subject matter; for example, a young people's picture book will look different from a school textbook.

A. How Do You Design a Book?

Keeping the subject matter in mind, think about how you want your book to look. Consider shape, size, and general appearance from an artistic point of view. Do you want a big rectangular book with chunky blocks of large type, bold colors, and wide margins (a)? Do you want a small square book with medium-sized margins and a few lines of type beneath each page of softly colored illustrations (b)? Would you prefer your book to be an unusual shape, such as a circle, cat silhouette, diamond, etc., instead of a rectangle (c)? *Note*: If you want a uniquely shaped book, be sure to keep the left edge straight so the book can be fastened with a spine following one of the methods described in Chapter IV.

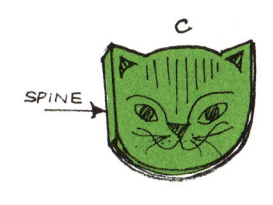

When designing a book, remember that you are combining many separate elements to make a single unit. All the parts must look related so that the total effect is one of unity. Imagine how it would look, for example, if the title of chapter one were in block letters and the title of chapter two were in script. Throughout the book—and on its cover and dust jacket—the illustrations and the text, whether handwritten or printed or typed, should be similar in style. Read Sections F and G of this chapter for details about illustration and text. If the illustrations are strong and bold, the type should be strong and bold. Delicate, fragile artwork is better suited to finer, light or medium-weight type.

The color of the page paper—be it white, off-white, or colored—should relate well the colors of the endpapers and book covers. The design and color of the illustrations should be coordinated with the design and color of the endpapers, covers, and dust jacket. Think about whether you want some pages full of type and others full of illustration, or illustrations scattered throughout the text. Do you want illustrations to keep within the text margins (a), or to *bleed* or "run off" the edges of the page (b)? Choose whichever style will best fit the text.

Now select your binding method following the suggestions in Chapter IV. When you have decided on the appearance and binding technique of your book, you are ready to arrange, or lay out, the text and illustrations on the pages of your *dummy* following the directions below. A dummy is a working model of your book, made up of blank pages on which you plan the *layout* of the type and illustrations, carefully condsidering margins, type style, and overall design for each page.

B. How Do You Make a Dummy?

1. Decide on the shape, page size, and binding method for your book. *Note*: The binding method of the dummy does *not* have to be the same one you will use for the book, but you should read through your binding directions to see if there are any special margin and endpaper requirements.

One way to make a dummy is to gather together a stack of single pages of the correct size and fasten them on the spine edge (the left side) with staples or paper fasteners (a). OR you may gather together a stack of *folded* pages following the directions for making a *signature* in Chapter VIII, Section B (b). The signature may or may not be stapled; it is *not* necessary to sew it together for the purposes of a dummy. Start the dummy with 8 to 16 pages; add more pages in *multiples of 4* until you have completed the book.

16

2. If your book's binding method requires endpapers and you want to decorate them, they may be added onto the dummy now. Leave them off the dummy if they will be plain, undecorated paper.

3. To plan the organization of *front* and *back matter* (title page, table of contents, etc.), read Chapter X. You will probably want to use a much simpler format than that found in most printed books; when you have read about what information should be included, you can make up your own arrangement. Be sure, however, to begin your book with a title page stating the title, author, and illustrator. Endpapers, if you use them, form the first and last pages of the dummy, so when you number the pages of your dummy, begin with the first page *after* the endpaper.

4. Read the rest of this chapter to learn about layout, illustration, and text. Then take your rough illustration sketches and the first draft of the text *or* pieces of blank, lined paper (to indicate writing), cut them to the size you want, and hold them in place on the dummy pages with paper clips. Move the pieces of paper around until you are sure you like the layout, then rubber-cement the pieces in place. Finally, you can add color with felt pens, colored pencils, or watercolors. Now follow the directions in Chapters IV through VIII for binding your real book. Use this dummy as your guide in placing the finished manuscript and artwork on the pages. You may do this either before or after completing the binding, depending on which method you choose from Chapter IV.

THIS LAYOUT ↑
BECOMES THIS ↓

C. How Do You Lay Out Pages?

Careful layout and design of margins, type, and artwork should make a page easy to read. The margins should neither be so narrow that the page overflows with type, nor so large that the type drowns in a sea of blank paper.

Generally, you need margins of *at least* ½" at the top, bottom, and sides of a page. Sometimes the bottom and fore-edge margins will be wider than the others, perhaps ¾". If you have only a small amount of type or a tiny illustration for a page, it is arranged just below the top margin, with the largest blank space at the bottom of the page. Some binding techniques require a wider left-side margin, so read binding directions carefully.

The *text*, or writing, should be neat and clear. The style, or "face," of the letters should be the same, or similar, throughout the book. Choose one style of printing, writing in script, or typing and stick to it. Of course, you will use upper and lower case (capital and small) letters, and you may wish to decorate initials (the first letter of a word) at the beginning of chapters. Titles and headings are usually a larger or more decorative form of type. Printed typefaces come in many styles, each having a different name, such as those shown at the right. If you handwrite your book, use whatever style is comfortable for you and still is clearly readable.

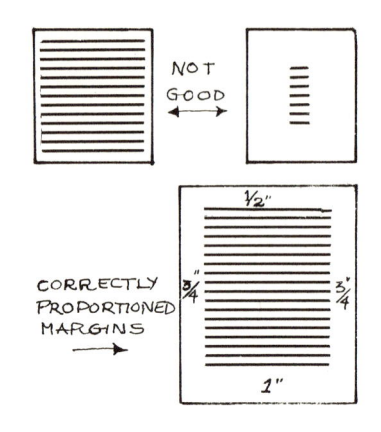

Palatino (12 pt.)

Palatino Italic (12 pt.)

BROADWAY (18 pt.)

Helvetica Bold (18 pt.)

Mistral (20 pt.)

Windsor Outline (18 pt.)

(36 pt. Caslon Initial)

D. How Is the Text Placed in the Bound Book?

After you have corrected the first draft of your manuscript, decided on the book's design, margins, and type style, and made a dummy, you can plan the layout of text areas on each page, as in step 4 of Section B of this chapter. Then you will make the final manuscript, either by hand printing or writing in script with a pen or hard (nonsmudging) pencil or by typing. Use only one side of clean white or softly colored paper. (It is hard on the eyes to read type on very bright or very dark-colored papers.) If your paper is unlined, you may draw *light* pencil guidelines; or, rule very dark guidelines on a spare piece of book-size paper and slip this lined piece underneath each book page as you write—the lines will show through to guide you. Also draw light margin lines on the left and right edges of your pages to keep the text straight. Erase the guidelines—if penciled on the pages—when you have completed the writing. The best eraser is a soft "kneaded" rubber or art gum eraser, neither of which will damage your paper.

You may place the text in the book in one of three ways. In all cases use the dummy as your guide to placement. (1) You can bind together the blank pages of the book and then print or write the text *directly* onto the pages as described above. Use the final manuscript as your model. Or, (2) you can bind together the blank pages of the book and then *cut up* your final manuscript into pieces as indicated by the dummy and rubber-cement the pieces into place on the bound book's pages. (3) Prepare the pages of your book as if it were going to be bound. BUT *do not* sew or otherwise fasten the pages together. At this stage, number the pages to keep them in order. Add the text and illustrations to the pages as in (1) or (2). Finally, bind all pages together. The last two methods are the easiest and safest, for corrections can be made by simply replacing a piece of paper rather than spoiling a bound page.

E. Should You Number the Pages of Your Book?

For ease in planning, it is helpful to number the pages of the dummy. In your bound book, you may or may not want to use page numbers. Page numbers in a bound book are called *folios*. If you use folios, they may be placed above or below the block of text or illustrations, in any *one* of the several positions shown. The location you select should be the one which makes the book easiest to use.

As you will see here, the folio is either centered on or in line with the outer margin of the text. Be consistent and place the folio in the same position on every page. Remember that the folio is only a guide, and should be small so it does not look more important than the text.

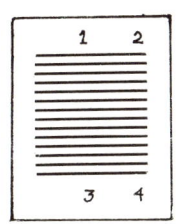

F. How Do You Plan the Illustrations?

Book illustration is really a part of book design. Being the author, you already know the book well and have given some thought to what you want it to look like. Now, read through the manuscript to see which scenes or ideas seem most picturesque or most in need of explanatory pictures. Make notes to yourself in the margins of the first or second *rough* draft (not the final copy). Think about how the text makes you feel. Bright and gay? Somber and sad? Soft and quiet? Choose a technique and colors that will best complement the feeling of the text. For example, bold, wide felt-pen lines with bright colors might go well with a happy circus story, while delicate pen lines and a wash of pale watercolor would suit a mysterious fairy tale.

G. What Technique Should You Use for the Illustrations?

Illustrations may be paintings, drawings, prints, photographs, or collages cut out of pieces of colored paper, magazines, etc. and pasted down (see Section H of this chapter). If you need inspiration in planning your illustrations, go to the library and look through books on the

LINOLEUM BLOCK PRINT

PEN AND INK

PEN AND INK AND COLLAGE

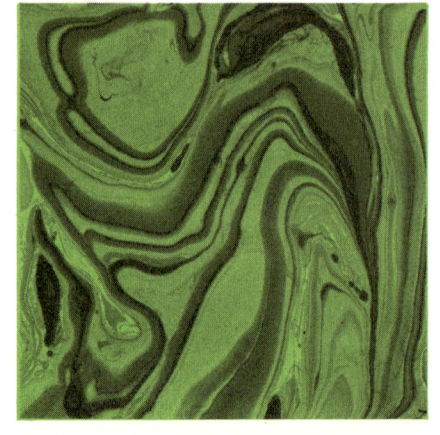

MARBLEIZED PAPER

same or related subjects. You will not want to copy someone else's work, but you will surely find ideas to help you get started.

The main restriction on method of artwork is that the medium used must not rub off easily, or the pages will smear. Therefore, soft pastel chalk and charcoal are not really suitable, although they can be used if they are "fixed" (sprayed with fixative found in a hardware or art store). You will have best results using pencils, wax crayons, pen and ink, watercolor, tempera, water-based felt or nylon-tipped pens . . . any nonsmudging technique. (*Note*: Some oil-base felt pens and paints "bleed" or come through the paper, showing on the back side. If you wish to use these materials, you must do your artwork on separate paper and then glue it onto the bound book's pages.)

You can make prints out of linoleum blocks, erasers, potatoes, beans, string, or your hands; you can "marbleize" your endpapers in the manner of fine European handmade books. Details and directions for these techniques can be found in one of my previous books, HOLIDAY CARDS FOR YOU TO MAKE (Lippincott, 1967). Decorative endpapers and book covers can be made of tie-dyed soft papers or fabrics; see my COSTUMES FOR YOU TO MAKE (Lippincott, 1971). Illustrations may be done on white page paper or on colored art papers (see Chapter V).

H. How Do You Actually Illustrate?

To get an idea of the style as well as the number of illustrations, first go through your original planning notes. Then make rough sketches on any type of paper, in line, with or without color. It is not necessary to use the same technique you will use finally. Try to make these sketches the correct size to fit on your book's pages even though they may later be made bigger or smaller. Use the sketches to plan the layout of your dummy according to step 4 of Section B of this chapter. Paper-clip, then rubber-cement the sketches in place on the pages of the dummy.

You may illustrate the finished book in one of two ways. In either case, use the dummy as your guide to placement. (1) You can do your finished artwork *directly* on the pages of the book—before or after it is bound—or (2) the finished artwork may be done on *separate* paper, cut out, and rubber-cemented in place on the bound book's pages. This last method is the safest, for you can easily replace any illustrations that you don't like, or one that gets spoiled.

IV. WHAT KIND OF BINDING SHOULD YOU USE?

Bookbinders use several different binding methods. The one you select will depend on the length of your manuscript, the amount of time and effort you wish to spend, and how durable and professional-looking you want your book to be. The descriptions below will help you make your binding selection.

Materials needed for binding are listed in Chapter V and before each separate section. Special binding skills are described in Chapter VI. These techniques and the special bookbinder's terms (Chapter II) should be noted before you begin. Also be sure to read all binding directions through to the end before you start work so that you will be able to plan your materials and your time.

The easiest and quickest methods of binding short manuscripts using single, unfolded pages with flexible paper covers are:

Stapled Binding (may also be used with folded pages). See Chapter VII, Section A.

Brass Fastener Binding. See Chapter VII, Section B.

Sewn Binding. See Chapter VII, Section C.

STAPLED    BRASS FASTENER    SEWN

To bind any number of single, unfolded pages between stiff covers (cardboard covered with decorative paper), use:

Single Sheets Sewn to Hinged Boards (Chapter VIII, Section A).

This method takes a little more time and effort than the first three but the result is very attractive and, with the flexible hinge, it looks rather like a fine hand-bound Japanese book.

If you prefer to fold large sheets of paper in half to make your pages, these may be gathered together and sewn in groups which, you will remember from Chapter II, are called signatures. Signatures are always in multiples of 4. For a book of up to 32 pages, use:

Single-Signature Book, Sewn (Chapter VIII, Section B). Decorate the outer sheet to make the book's cover. This is the simplest sewn method for a fairly short book.

Single-Signature Book, Half-Bound (Chapter VIII, Section C). This has paper-covered boards with tape spine and corner covers. It requires more time and effort than the sewn single signature book above, but it is more durable and professional-looking.

Books of more than 32 pages sewn in signatures may be:

Multi-Signature Book, Full-Bound with Case (Chapter VIII, Section D).

With this method, the pages are fastened to a cardboard case (Chapter II) covered with decorative material. This is not difficult to do, but it takes more time and patience than the other methods. The result is quite elegant and well worth the trouble.

Note: To repair torn or worn-out bindings on printed books in your own library, carefully cut off the old cover boards and replace them with half- or full-case bindings as described above. Treat the sewn pages of your old book as you would the newly made signatures. Repair torn pages with matte-finish transparent tape.

V. MATERIALS LIST

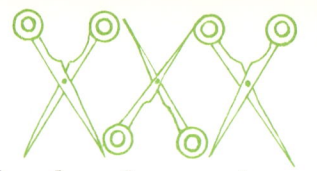

Although professional hand-bookbinders use special tools and unusual materials such as handmade papers, vegetable glues, soft leathers, and gold leaf, we will use simple, everyday materials that you will have readily available. The following is a list of all the materials used in this book, although each binding technique will require only a few items at a time. You should be able to locate all your materials around your home and school, local stationery, art supply, or variety shop, fabric or hardware store. If you have trouble finding anything, or if you wish to purchase professional equipment, look in the Yellow Pages of the telephone book, under Bookbinders' Equipment & Supplies.

- ruler, preferably with metal edge
- paper clips
- pencil, colored pencil, felt pens
- chalk: regular blackboard chalk or tailor's chalk found in fabric stores
- crayons, watercolors, tempera paints, etc. (for illustrating techniques and materials, see Chapter III, Sections G and H)
- scissors
- pushpins
- nails: 2 or 3, about 3" long with heads
- stapler and staples
- brass paper fasteners
- beeswax (optional): a 2" block, available in hobby and candle-making shops
- utility or X-Acto knife: if possible, use X-Acto knife with a safety shield, and #11 blade
- masking tape, cellophane tape, Mystik cloth tape
- rubber cement or white glue: excess rubber cement can be rubbed off any surface, and is easier to work with than white glue, which dries clear but is still visible on a binding. White glue may be slightly diluted with water and brushed onto cardboard before covering with fabric.
- darning or embroidery needle with sharp point
- rubber bands: large size, about 3" unstretched
- large old magazine, scrap cardboard, or wood plank for protective table cover
- iron (for pressing fabric)

wooden mallet, block of wood, or hammer

sewing material: cotton button thread, or double thickness of #30 or #40 cotton thread, or wool, or multistrand embroidery thread, or string, or ribbon

wax paper or clean scrap paper: do not use printed newsprint as the ink sometimes rubs off on glued surfaces

erasers: kneaded rubber or art gum, found in art, stationery, and hobby shops

cardboard: for cover boards, use illustration board, mat board, chip board, all approximately 1/16" to 1/8" thick, found in art supply stores

page paper: any bond or typing or 3-ring notebook paper, or strong, smooth-surfaced rice paper (do not write text directly on this in ink unless you test it for blurring first). Paper may lined or unlined

board-covering paper: any flexible paper which does not crack when folded and has a fairly durable surface, such as gift-wrapping paper. Imported Italian or French hand-made and/or hand-printed papers, wallpaper (you can often locate free out-of-date sample books in decorating or wallpaper stores), art papers like vellum, bond, or charcoal, and self-adhesive decorating or shelf paper

board-covering fabrics: any fairly close-woven material you find around the house—worn-out curtain or upholstery fabric (if not too thick), old dress or blue jeans cloth, drapery remnants. Cotton and linen are easiest to work with, but remember that very loose weaves are unsuitable because they tend to pull at angles against the grain. You may also use fake leathers, plastic, suede or suede cloth

VI. BASIC SKILLS

Note: Throughout this book, the symbol ″ means inches, and ′ means feet.

A. How to Cut a Straight Edge on Paper or Cardboard

If you are careful you can cut straight edges on paper with scissors. However, an X-Acto or utility knife held against a metal-edged ruler will always give you a dependable and neat edge on both paper and cardboard. THE KNIFE IS SHARP AND SHOULD NOT BE USED WITHOUT AN ADULT'S SUPERVISION.

1. Use a ruler and pencil to lightly mark the lines to be cut—on paper or cardboard.

2. Protect cutting surface by covering it with an old magazine, heavy cardboard, or scrap wood. Set paper (not more than 2 or 3 pieces at a time) or cardboard (only 1 piece at a time) on cutting surface. Hold ruler firmly down against the marked line. Carefully run the knife along the ruler's edge, pressing down evenly so the cut can be made in one single stroke to avoid jagged edges. If a second cut must be made, be sure to set the knife precisely in the previously cut line. KEEP YOUR FINGERS WELL AWAY FROM THE KNIFE'S PATH.

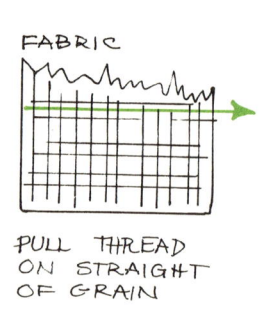

PULL THREAD ON STRAIGHT OF GRAIN

B. How to Cut Fabric "on the Grain"

In many of the following binding techniques, woven material (cotton, linen, etc.) may be substituted for paper. If you do this, be sure the fabric is ironed flat before you measure it. Also be sure you measure, and cut, along the "straight of the grain," following the direction of the threads and not working on a slant. Chalk marks cloth more easily than pencil, and will brush off later. Trim any jagged or uneven edges of fabric before beginning to work. In loosely woven cloth, you can pull a single cross thread to find the straight grain as shown.

C. How to Fold Paper "on the Grain"

The *grain* is the primary direction of the fibers making up the paper. When folding paper, you will find that it will lie flatter and make a neater folded edge if folded *with* the grain rather than against it. With thin papers, such as typing paper, grain is not too important. However, for heavier-weight papers used for folded signature pages (Chapter VIII, Section B), and for cover material and dust jackets (Chapter IX, Section B), folding with the grain is an important factor determining the neatness of your work.

To find the direction of the grain, place a sheet of your paper flat on the table. Pull one edge of the paper over to meet the other—but do not fold. If the grain (arrows, a) runs in the *same* direction as your turned edge, the paper will tend to stay flapped over and when you press it down you will feel that it could be folded easily along this edge. This is the correct direction for your fold.

If you pull one edge of the paper over and it tends to spring back up, and if you have difficulty making a neat fold along this edge, then the grain runs *against* the direction of your turned edge (b). Repeat both these tests, pressing along the turned edge to make a fold: a neat even line goes *with* the grain; an uneven, rough fold goes *against* the grain.

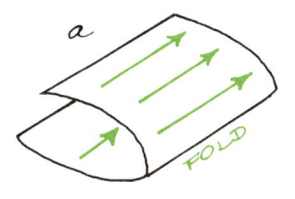

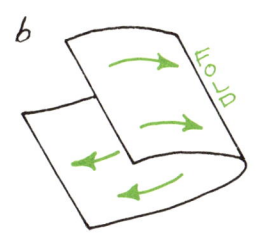

D. How to Strengthen Cotton Sewing Thread

Pull the required length of regular cotton button thread through the edge of a block of beeswax (see Chapter V) so that the thread is thoroughly coated. Brush off any large lumps of wax which stick to the thread. Then sew with the thread as you normally would.

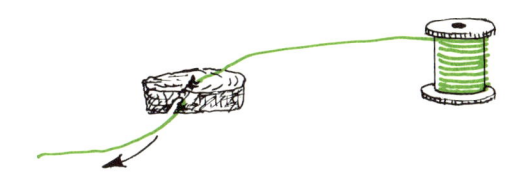

E. Hole-Measuring Guides for Sewn Bindings

Materials: Any lightweight, flexible paper (bond, typing, etc.), ruler, pencil, scissors.

General Directions: See Chapter III, Section A, to select your book's shape and size, and see Chapter IV to select your binding method. A book up to 6″ high uses a 3-hole sewn binding; a taller book may use a 3-hole or a 5-hole, depending on its size. Always cut the hole-measuring guide as wide as is specified on your binding directions and as high as the book's cover board. Both these measurements are given in the binding directions which follow.

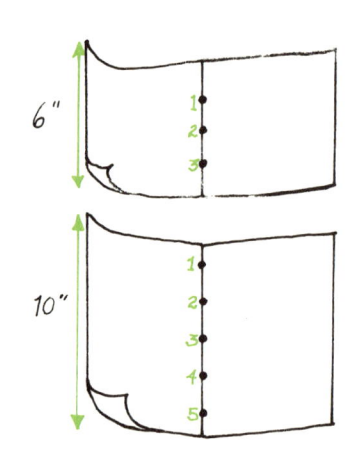

1. 3-Hole Guide

Note: Our example will be a strip ¾″ by 6″, but this system will work for a strip of any dimensions. a) First, cut a paper strip as wide as your directions specify (¾″) and as high as the cover board (6″). Bring the *long* sides of the strip together, folding it in half lengthwise. Press along fold, then open flat.

b) To divide the strip into thirds: first bring the *short* ends together and fold the strip in half crosswise; press on fold. When you open the strip flat, you will see the mark left by the fold. Bring the left short end over to that center fold mark, and press it flat. Repeat with the right short end.

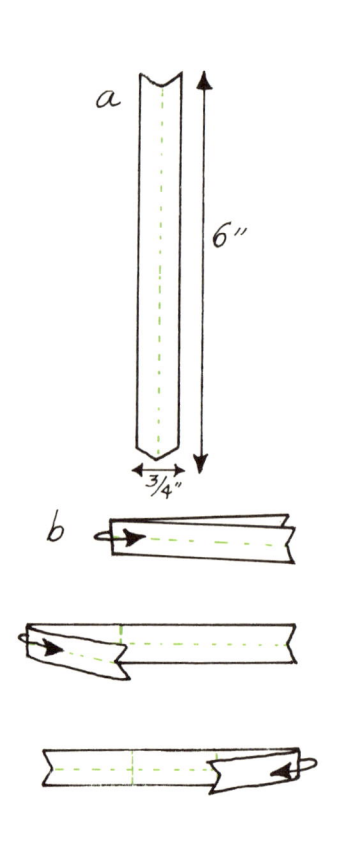

c) Open strip flat. You will see 3 points where the cross folds meet the lengthwise fold. Make a pencil dot at each of these 3 points to mark the stitch holes. Then, with a sharp pencil point, carefully poke a hole in the paper through each dot. As a guide to yourself, number the holes as shown.

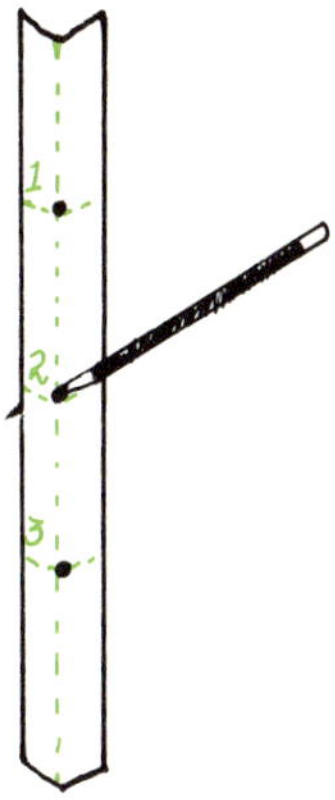

2. 5-Hole Guide

a) For strip's dimensions, see 3-Hole Guide, step a. In this example, the strip is ¾" by 10¼". First, measure and mark off points ¾" in from each short end of the strip as shown. Then fold the strip in half lengthwise, press along fold, and open it flat.

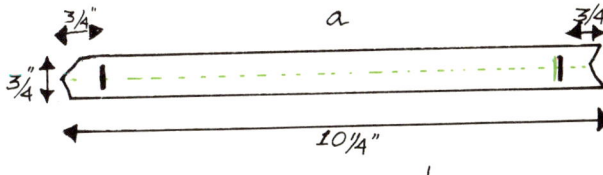

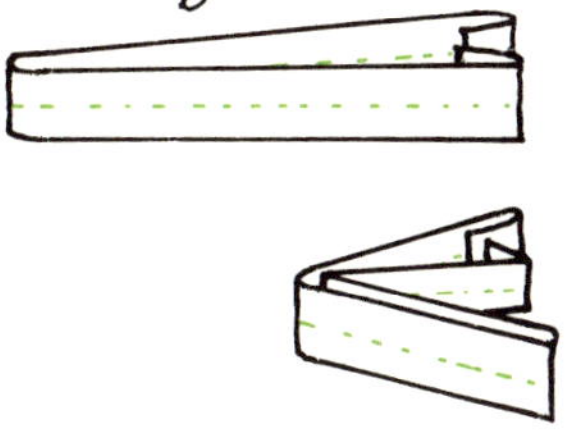

b) Fold up each short end at the ¾" mark. Then bring folded short ends together, folding strip in half crosswise. Fold it in half once more, dividing it in quarters. Press on folds.

c) Open the strip flat and look for the 5 points where the cross folds meet the lengthwise fold. Make a pencil dot at each of these 5 points to mark the stitch holes. Then, with a sharp pencil point, carefully poke a hole in the paper through each dot. As a guide to yourself, number the holes as shown.

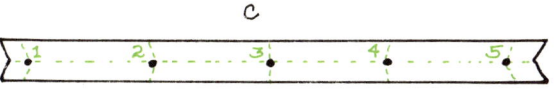

F. Sewing Methods

Materials: Cotton button thread, or string, or wool, or several strands of embroidery or darning thread, or twine or macrame string, long darning needle, ruler or tape measure, 3 paper clips, scissors.

General Directions: Cut your thread or string as long as it is specified in your binding directions (about twice as long as the book's cover board is high). If using cotton thread, pull it through beeswax (Chapter VI, Section D) to strengthen it. Thread the darning needle and tie one end of the thread—about 3″—very loosely onto a paper clip. Follow the directions in Section E of this chapter to make a 3- or 5-hole measuring guide for your sewing. Then paper-clip the hole guide onto the front of the paper or board to be sewn. Mark the holes, then remove the hole guide. With book's pages held firmly together by paper clips or rubber bands, stitch through the holes as follows:

1. 3-Hole Sewing Method

Sew down into the center hole (a, #2). The paper clip will keep the thread end from pulling through the hole. Then sew up into hole #1, and *skipping* center hole, sew down into hole #3. Then sew up into center hole #2.

Untie thread from paper clip. Pull thread ends taut, then tie thread ends together over the long top thread. Tie thread into a decorative knot or bow. Thread ends may be frayed (b), or tied into neat knots to avoid fraying (c).

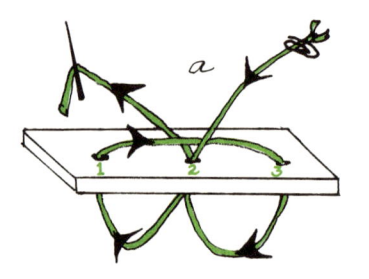

2. 5-Hole Sewing Method

Cut thread to the length specified in binding directions. Sew down through center hole #3 so paper clip catches the thread and keeps it from pulling through. Sew up through hole #2, down through #1, back up again into #2, over top *skipping* hole #3 and down into #4, up into #5, down into #4 again, then up into center hole #3.

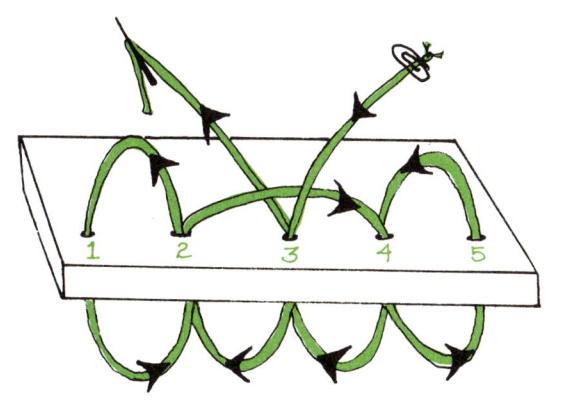

Untie thread from paper clip. Pull all thread loops taut, following directions of arrows. Tie thread ends together over the long thread between holes #2 and #4. Tie a bow or decorative knot and finish as in 3-Hole Sewing Method, (b) or (c).

VII. SIMPLE BINDINGS

These three methods are the easiest and quickest ways to bind short books having single, unfolded pages, or folded pages, and flexible paper covers.

Materials: Page and cover paper (see Chapter V), stapler or brass paper fasteners or darning needle and sewing material (thread, wool, etc.), pencil, ruler, scissors or utility knife, wooden mallet or block of wood, large old magazine or protective table covering, paper clips.

A. Stapled Binding
Method 1
This is the easiest and best way to bind single, unfolded pages and covers of construction, art, or manila paper. Do not use it if your covers are made of stiff cardboard.

a) Cut pages to the correct size, or use precut paper such as typing paper. Cut cover papers the same size as pages or ¼″ larger at head, fore-edge and foot edges. Or, you can use a cover sheet at least twice as large as your paper, and fold it in half at the spine. Decorate front cover now. Complete text and artwork (see Chapter III).

b) Gather all the pages together inside the cover sheets. Line up all edges (if you have a folded cover, line up left page edges tight to fold) and hold them in place with paper clips as shown.

c) With front cover facing up, staple down along the spine an even distance in from the edge. To guide you in stapling evenly, you may want to measure about 1″ in from the spine edge and draw a few *light* pencil dots to follow.

Method 2

Use for *folded* pages and a *folded* paper cover.

a) Measure, cut, and fold all pages in half. Writing and illustrating may be completed at this time or after binding is finished (see Chapter III). Measure and cut cover paper either the same size as an opened page or about ¼" larger all around. Decorate front of cover now.

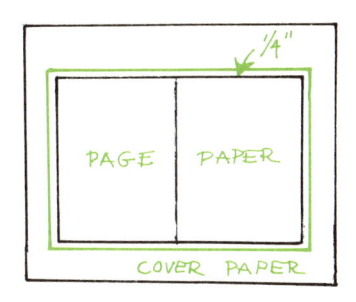

b) Gather all pages together in proper order, and set pages inside folded cover. All folded edges are now at left to form the spine. Open book carefully to *center* page. Paper-clip both pages and cover together with all edges lined up neatly; if cover is slightly larger than page size, there should be an even border showing all around pages.

c) Place a protective covering on table. Turn paper-clipped book over, with its cover facing up, on work area. Open your stapler so it is *unhinged* (an adult can show you how to do this if you find it difficult). Hold stapler as shown, so the staples will be placed vertically down along the center fold of cover. You need to use only three or four staples. Set the stapler head in line with the fold and press sharply, causing the staples to go through the cover and the pages and stick into the protective covering on the table below. When all staples are in place, carefully lift the book *straight up*, without disturbing the staples, and turn it over so that the center page faces up.

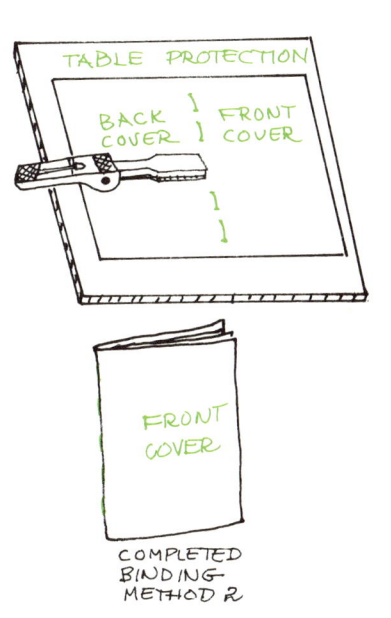

d) You will see the staple ends sticking straight up through the fold. Use the end of a pencil or the edge of a ruler to press staples closed. When all staples are bent over, binding is complete.

B. Brass Fastener Binding *Method 1*

Use 3-hole notebook paper (or other paper with *precut holes*).

a) To make the cover, fold in half 1 sheet of cover paper that is at least twice the size of your page paper, or use 2 sheets of cover paper. Cut cover either the same size as the page paper or ¼" larger on 3 sides. If you use 2 cover sheets, paper-clip front and back covers together, edges lined up; if you use 1, make sure it is folded exactly in half.

b) To mark fastener holes, place a sheet of notebook paper on top of front cover with holes at left side, left edges lined up exactly, leaving ¼" border around other 3 sides. With pencil, mark through the 3 holes. Remove notebook paper, paper-clip front and back covers together, set them on old magazine or other table covering, and poke through the hole marks with paper punch, darning needle, pencil, utility knife, or scissors tip. Do not tear paper. Now decorate front cover.

c) Complete writing and illustrating of book's pages. Gather pages together in proper order, place them between front and back covers. If you have used 2 sheets, make sure the left edges are lined up. For one sheet folded in half, make sure the fold is on the left and the left edges of all the pages are lined up against the fold. Allow an even border about ¼" wide around 3 other sides. Push brass fasteners through holes from the front cover through the pages and the back cover. Then spread apart the fasteners' legs so they lie flat. Binding is complete.

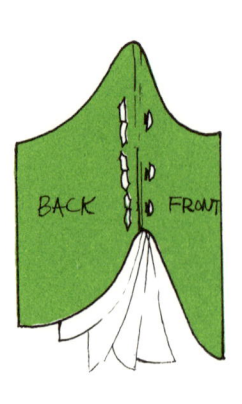

34

Method 2
Use when you have single-sheet pages *without* precut holes.

a) Make a Hole-Measuring Guide as in Chapter VI, Section E. Your guide may be 1" wide and as long as your page paper, and may have either 3 or 5 holes.

b) Cut or fold cover paper as in Method 1, step a. Decorate front cover. Complete writing and illustrating pages. Gather pages together in proper order, place them between front and back covers with left edges lined up and ¼" border around 3 other sides. Paper-clip all pages together, and then paper-clip the hole-measuring guide to the left edge as shown. Set it on your protective table covering. Mark through the guide holes with a pencil. Then, cut out the holes with a paper punch. Or, use a darning needle, nail, pushpin, or other pointy object to poke through each hole. Or, hammer a darning needle, nail, or pushpin with a block of wood or a mallet, poking through each hole and into the protective table covering. Remove hole-measuring guide, but leave other paper clips in while you place a brass fastener in each hole. Make sure that the round heads of the fasteners all appear on the front cover, and that the legs are spread apart on the back cover. Now remove the paper clips. Your book is complete.

COMPLETE BINDING

C. Sewn Binding

The technique is the same as for the Brass Fastener Binding, Method 1 or 2, only instead of using brass fasteners in the holes, sew through them with wool, string, or ribbon. See sewing directions in Chapter VI, Section F.

VIII. OTHER BINDINGS

A. Single Sheets Sewn to Hinged Boards

This method of binding is used to fasten precut, unfolded, single pages between hinged cardboard covers. *Note*: When planning the inside pages of your book, allow a 1½″ *left* margin to accommodate the hinge fastening.

Materials: Cardboard for covers (see Chapter V), chalk, ruler, pencil, utility knife, scissors, masking tape, rubber cement, wax paper, cotton or linen cloth, colored decorative paper (for endpapers and for cover paper), paper clips, large rubber bands, scrap paper, 2 nails and hammer, 2 pieces of scrap cardboard or scrap wood plank slightly larger than the size of your book, darning needle, and wool or thread.

1. To make the pages of the book, use typing paper or any other precut paper, or cut your own sheets to the size you prefer. Measure the page size. In our example, the pages are 8″ wide by 10″ high. To make the front and back covers, cut 2 pieces of cardboard the *same* width (8″) as the page and ¼″ more than page height (10″ plus ¼″ = 10¼″). Place protective covering of scrap cardboard or wood on table. Then measure, mark, and draw a line ¾″ in from one long side of each board (a). On each board, cut along this line using a utility knife and a metal-edged ruler (see Chapter VI, Section A). *Be careful when using the knife.* You will now have two *hinge strips* each ¾″ wide by 10¼″ high (A) and two boards (B) each 7¼″ by 10¼″ (b).

2. To make a measuring guide for the binding's hinge, cut 2 pieces of cover-type cardboard about 2″ by 2″ each. Tape them together side by side. Set this aside for the moment.

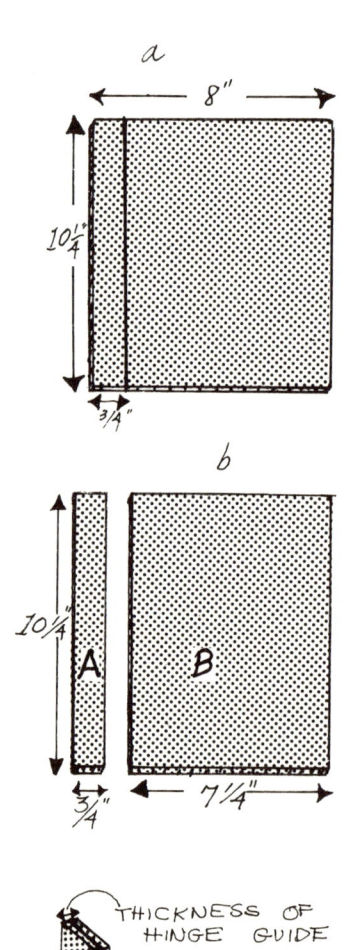

36

3. Both boards (B) may now be covered with decorative paper or cloth. Set covering material wrong side up on the table and tape down the edges with masking tape. Set 1 board over the material, hold it down firmly with one hand or tape the corners, and draw around board's edges with pencil if the covering material is paper, with chalk if the covering material is cloth. Remove board. Then measure ¾" outside this drawn edge and make a second rectangle as shown. Place the measuring guide you made in step 2 against each corner of the *inner* rectangle (arrow), mark its thickness, then draw an angle outside this mark on each corner. This should give you a space of about ⅛" between the inner corners and the angles. Cut around the *outer* rectangle and cut off the angles.

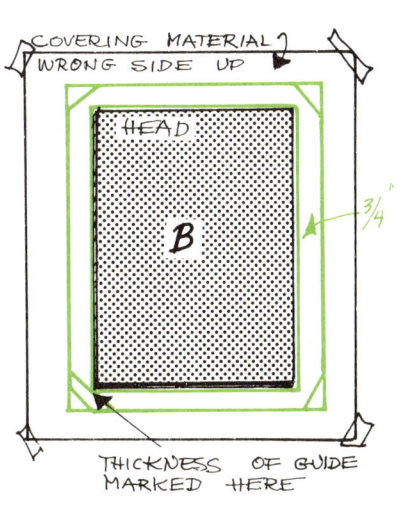

NOTE: IF COVERING MATERIAL PATTERN HAS DEFINITE TOP AND BOTTOM, COVER ONE BOARD B WITH PATTERN TOP AT HEAD EDGE, AND SECOND BOARD B WITH PATTERN UPSIDE DOWN. PATTERNS WILL MATCH WHEN BINDING IS COMPLETE.

4. Place the cut material *wrong (marked) side up* on the table and again tape down edges. Spread the entire surface with an even coat of rubber cement. Then spread cement on one side of one board (B). Keeping board and paper *head edge up* as shown (a), carefully place board's edges —glued side down—onto the inner rectangle. Press glued surfaces together lightly. Then quickly turn board *right side up* (board facing down), and cover decorative material with a protective piece of wax paper. Pressing from center toward outer edges (arrows, b), smooth cover material flat. Remove and discard wax paper.

37

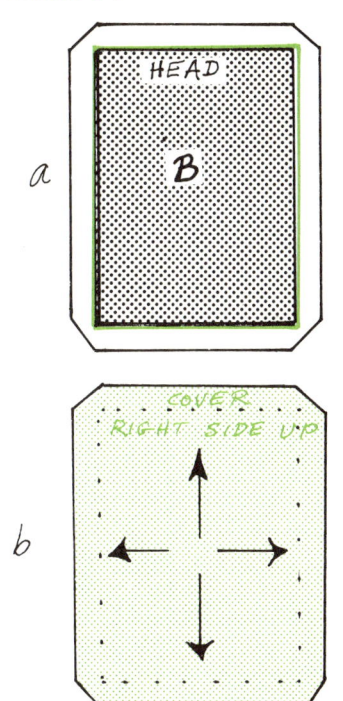

5. Turn board over so covered side is down. Spread rubber cement on inner surfaces of all flaps of cover material and on all sides and edges of the board. Pull *head* and *foot* (not side) flaps *up*; press them firmly against board edges, then pull them *over* and press them *down* onto board's surface (a). Rub flaps firmly onto board. At top and bottom corners, fold over a neat angle in each side flap as shown (b), fitting the folded angle tightly against the board's corner; use a fingernail or darning needle to press angle tight. Then spread glue on side flaps again (#3 and #4, c). Pull each side flap over and press down as you did the head and foot flaps. Numbers indicate the order of turning over flaps. Note that the turned-over side flaps meet the head and foot flaps in neat corners as shown (d). Don't worry if your angles are uneven; they will be covered by endpapers. Repeat steps 3, 4, and 5 to cover second board.

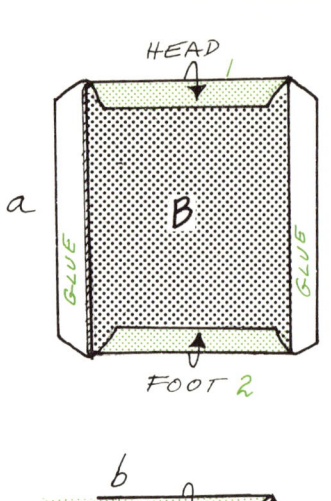

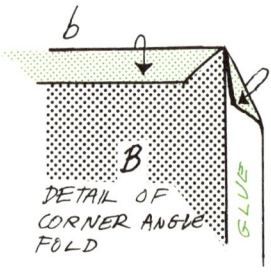

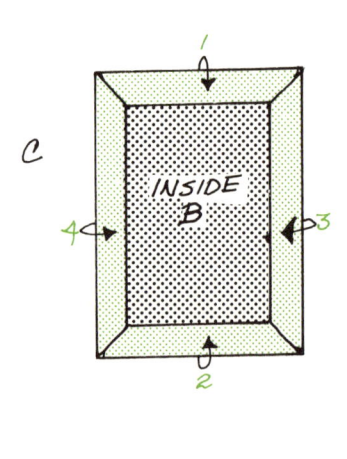

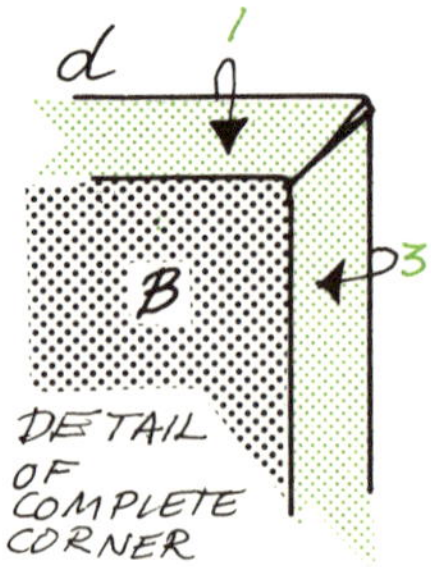

6. Hinges are covered with cloth, never with paper. To prepare hinge cloths, cut *with the grain* 2 cloth strips each 1" higher than board B (10¼" plus 1" = 11¼") and 4" wide. Be sure all cut edges are straight and square. *Wrinkled cloth should be ironed flat before measuring and cutting.*

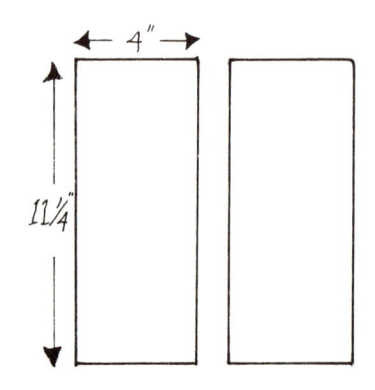

38

7. Set cloth strips *wrong side up* and measure, mark, and draw chalk margin lines ½" in from short ends. If cloth is a loose weave that tends to unravel at the cut edges, you must fold under the one long edge that will show on front and back boards; this will give boards a neat appearance. To do this, fold over and iron down onto the wrong side a border about ¼" wide on one long edge of each piece. *Note*: Pinking shears cut cloth so it does not unravel.

8. Fold one hinge cloth in half lengthwise, *wrong side out*. Fold is at left, and the turned-under border (if you have one) must be under the bottom layer (arrow). Tape cloth to table at top and bottom edges. Spread a border of rubber cement about ¾" wide alongside the fold edge (x's). Spread cement all over one side of the ¾"-wide cardboard hinge strip A. Leaving ½" of cloth overhanging both top and bottom of strip A, line up the left long edge of strip A with cloth fold and press glued surfaces together.

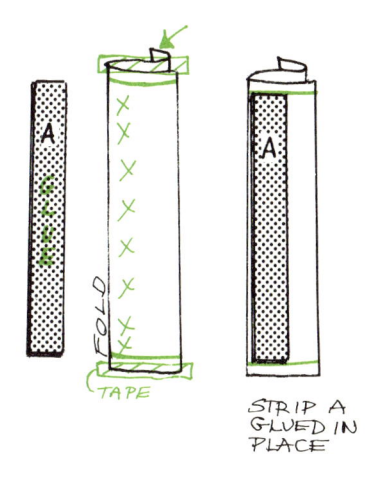

9. Take the 2-board measuring guide you made in step 2, and hold it firmly against the *right* edge of strip A (arrow). Mark boards' thickness with pencil or chalk; mark several times all the way along the side of strip A (dotted hinge line).

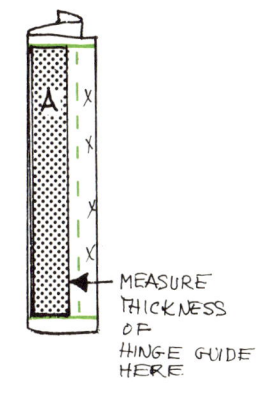

39

10. Spread rubber cement over surface of hinge cloth which remains facing you (x's, step 9). Turn cover board B (which already has been covered with decorative material) *wrong side up* and spread rubber cement in a 1¼"-wide strip against its *spine edge* (in example, that is one of the long edges). Then reverse board B so it is now *covered side up*, and keep it just above the surface of the cloth so it does not touch. Carefully line up left glued board edge with dotted hinge line *and* with the top and bottom margin lines drawn on the cloth. When edges are lined up as shown (a), press board B down in place. To smooth cloth onto the board, carefully turn both board and hinge over (b) *cloth side up*. Cover cloth with a piece of protective wax paper. Following arrows, gently smooth cloth onto board *and* onto hinge strip A, flattening any wrinkles. *Note*: Don't rub *too* hard or boards will slip.

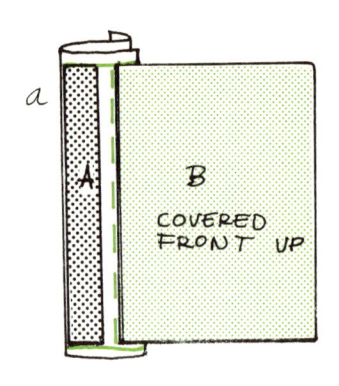

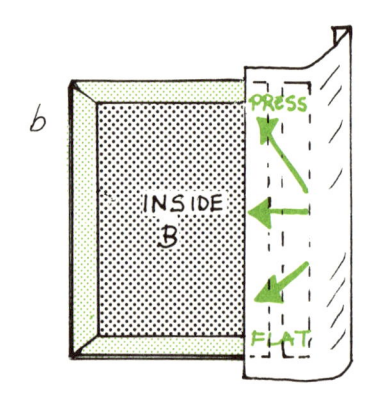

11. Turn boards over again, *cloth side down*, head edge at top. Unfold hinge cloth as shown. Make a short snip into the ½" top and bottom margins at points X and Y, exactly even with *left* edge of strip A. Brush cement over these margins Z, then fold them over onto boards A and B and smooth flat. Also spread cement all over strip A and over about a 1" border (v's) on hinge cloth just to left of strip A as shown.

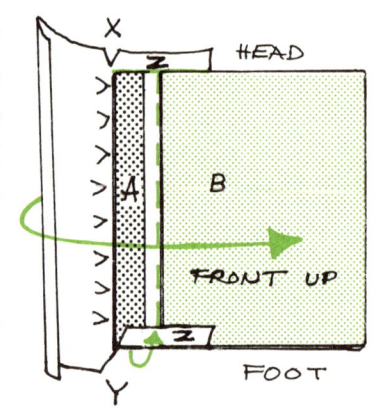

12. Gently pull outside edge of cloth over toward board B (colored arrow, step 11). Press cloth smoothly over onto hinge strip A. Brush rubber cement into the hinge space, then press cloth down onto it, smoothing it flat. Be sure to keep hinge space between boards A and B an even width. Press down into space with fingertip or pencil eraser. Brush a 1″ border of cement over inside spine edge of board B, and also on *inside* surface of remaining cloth. Press remaining cloth down onto board, smoothing flat from center toward edges. Cloth should be protected with a piece of wax paper while rubbing.

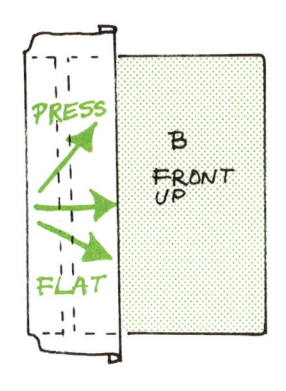

13. Turn boards over, *wrong side up*; ½″ hinge cloth margins now overhang head and foot edges of boards. Cut off margin corners X and Y as shown (a). Then rubber-cement margins down firmly onto hinge cloth (arrows, b). Repeat steps 8–13 to make cloth-covered hinge on second board B.

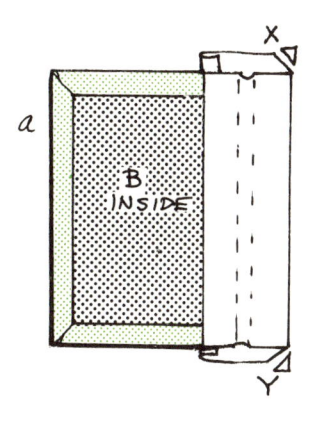

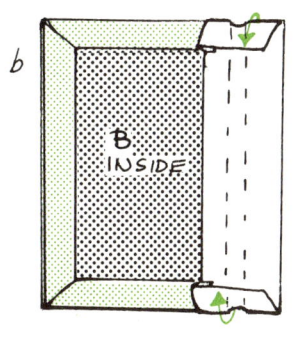

14. The inside surfaces of both boards B must now be covered with endpapers so that your binding will have a neatly finished interior. Endpapers cover all the inside of boards B except for a ⅛″ border all around the edges. Endpaper measurements, therefore, are ⅛″ smaller all around than the boards *without the hinges*; in our example, each board is 7¼″ by 10¼″. Subtracting ⅛″ from head and foot and each side, we find that the endpapers should each be cut to 7″ by 10″. Remember that endpaper colors should go well with cover and hinge design.

15. Prepare boards for covering with endpapers: Set one board as shown, wrong side up, hinge to left. Measure and mark head and fore-edges of board ⅛″ in from edge (green dotted line, a). Cut a piece of wax paper slightly larger than board; wax paper helps position the endpaper by keeping the 2 glued surfaces from touching. Spread rubber cement all over wrong side of board B and all over wrong side of endpaper (set all paper on scrap paper while spreading rubber cement). Place wax paper over glued board B, with head and fore-edges *just inside* the ⅛″ marks (b). Set endpaper—glued side down, head edge up—on top of wax paper. Move endpaper around until head and fore-edge are lined up exactly with the ⅛″ border lines (c). Check to see that endpaper sides are all parallel with board B edges. Then press down endpaper at head and fore-edge and carefully slip out wax paper from underneath. Lightly press glued surfaces together. Cut another piece of wax paper, set it on top of endpaper to protect it, and smooth endpaper onto board from center out (arrows, d). Repeat this step on second board B.

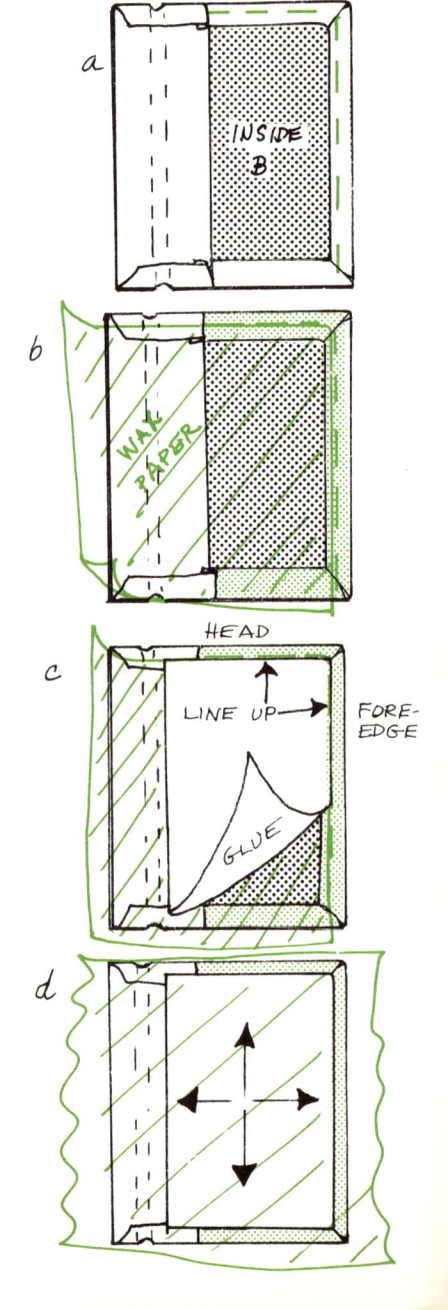

16. The hinge strip A of the *front* board will now be marked for the holes to be used in sewing the binding together. First, make a hole-measuring guide of 3 or 5 holes (depending on your book size) as described in Chapter VI, Section E. In our example, the 10¼"-high board uses 5 holes. The guide should be ¾" wide by 10¼" high. Set front board right side up, hinge at left. Paper-clip hole-measuring guide onto hinge strip A as shown, lining up edges evenly. Mark through each hole with sharp pencil or chalk. Remove strip.

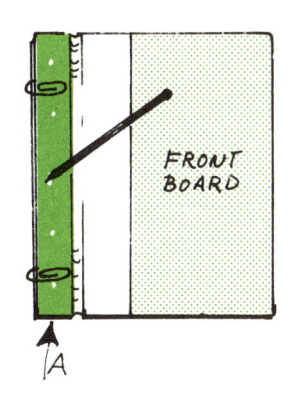

17. Complete writing and illustrating all pages of book. Gather all pages together in proper order. Even all edges by tapping stack's edge on tabletop. Fasten all pages together with paper clips (a) if book is not too thick, or a page-high strip of cardboard topped by a rubber band (b) if book is thick.

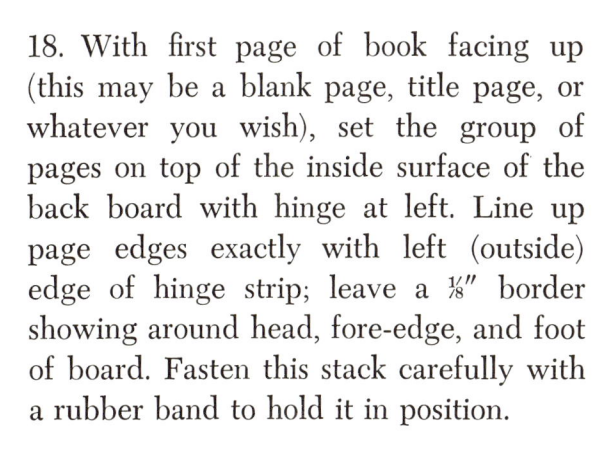

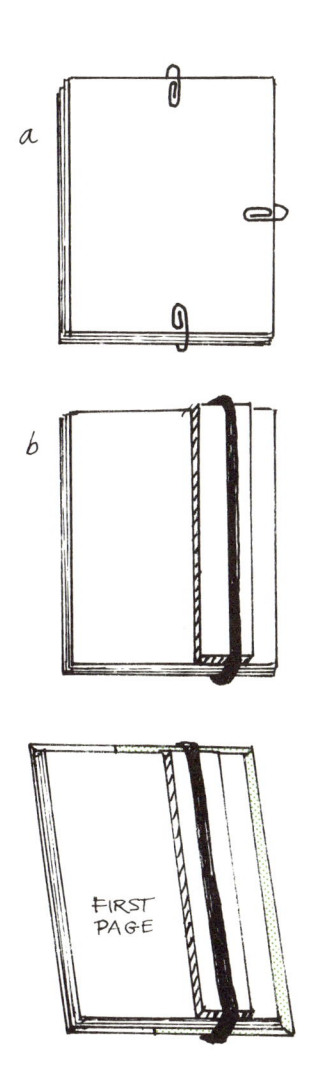

18. With first page of book facing up (this may be a blank page, title page, or whatever you wish), set the group of pages on top of the inside surface of the back board with hinge at left. Line up page edges exactly with left (outside) edge of hinge strip; leave a ⅛" border showing around head, fore-edge, and foot of board. Fasten this stack carefully with a rubber band to hold it in position.

19. Cover the stacked pages with the front board, its hinge at left lining up exactly with the left edges of the pages and bottom board. Fasten the whole book together with another rubber band. The pages are now sandwiched between the two cover boards. (If you think rubber bands may mark the cover paper, slip a piece of wax paper beneath the rubber band.)

20. Cover tabletop with protective piece of cardboard or wood. Set book—front cover up—on covered table. *Note*: If book is very thick, or you cannot hold it together with rubber bands, use a carpenter's "C" clamp and a strip of wood to fasten entire book down firmly to scrap wood set on table (a). Check to see that all edges are lined up evenly at left (hinge) edge and that a ⅛" margin of both boards extends evenly around the other 3 sides of the pages. Place nail in hole #1 (b) and hammer it until it goes through entire book and sticks into the protective board (*not the table*) below. With this nail in place, you can move boards or pages back into line in case they have slipped out of position. Leave first nail in place while using the second to stab through remaining holes. Remove nail each time by gently rocking it back and forth until it pulls out easily. Remove first nail last. Keep book held together with rubber bands and paper clips while sewing binding together (c) as described in Chapter VI, Section F. Remove book from "C" clamp, if you used that method, and fasten it with rubber band before sewing binding.

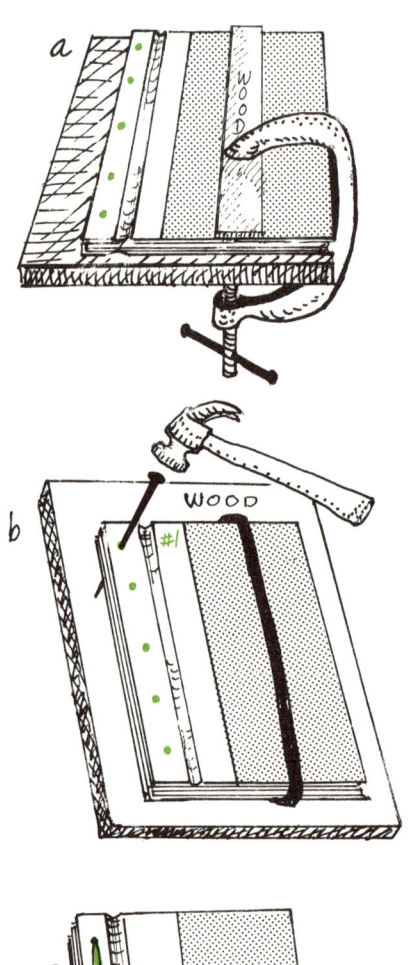

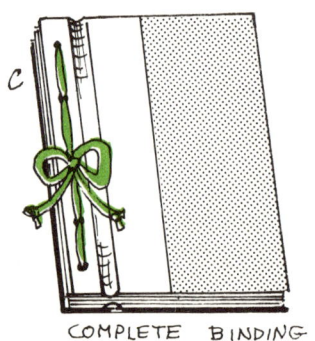

COMPLETE BINDING

B. Folding and Sewing a Single Signature

Unlike single-sheet books just discussed, a book made of signatures (or units) contains sheets of paper folded in half so each sheet has 4 sides—or pages. The signature received its name from the letter or mark placed on the first page of each section of a book or large printed sheet as a guide to the professional binder in folding and gathering (Chapter XI, Section G) the printed book. A signature usually contains 4 sheets, or 16 pages, and always contains pages in multiples of 4 (4, 8, 16, 32, 64, etc.) because the folded sheet or double-page unit has 4 sides. To better understand how this works, take a sheet of typing paper, fold it in half, then in half again, and you will have a small book of eight pages. If you neatly cut along one set of folded edges and leave the other folds for a spine, you will have a folded and trimmed sheet. If your book needs sixteen pages, you must take a second sheet, fold it into eight pages, and gather both units, or signatures, together. Your signature may have any number of sheets (4-page units) you like as long as the signature will not be too thick to close flat. For average-weight paper, 32 pages (2 signatures of 4 sheets each) is the maximum size you should fasten into a single unit for easy handling.

Materials: Page paper (see Chapter V), 2 rulers, masking tape, utility knife, scissors, darning needle and button thread, beeswax (optional), pencil, block of wood or mallet, paper clips or clamps, protective cardboard or wood covering for work table.

1. Decide on your *folded* page size. In the example, page is 7½″ wide and 10″ high; therefore, the sheet before folding will be twice as wide, or 15″, and the same height, 10″. Cut sheets correct size (see Chapter VI, Section A); fold them in half carefully. Press firmly along each folded edge with a ruler; this will help the pages lie flat. In addition to the number of pages you need for your text, add 2 more sheets (8 sides) on top of the others. These will be protective sheets; if you are making a cased-in or half-bound book, one of these extra sheets will be glued to the back board and the other will form the endpapers.

In our example, the text uses 16 pages all together (4 sheets having 4 sides, or pages, each) plus the 2 extra sheets, making a total of 6 sheets (24 pages). *Note*: To make a paper cover for a single-signature book, decorate the outside surface of the last sheet. The text and illustrations (including cover) can be completed now or after the signature is sewn together.

After all sheets are folded, stack them together in the proper order so when pages are turned they read like a book. Line up all edges; place signature flat open on table with the sheet that will be the *outer cover* or endpaper *facing up*. Paper-clip around all edges to hold pages together. Place stacked sheets on table; to guard against their slipping, place a ruler over each side of the top sheet and tape at top and bottom to the covered table as shown.

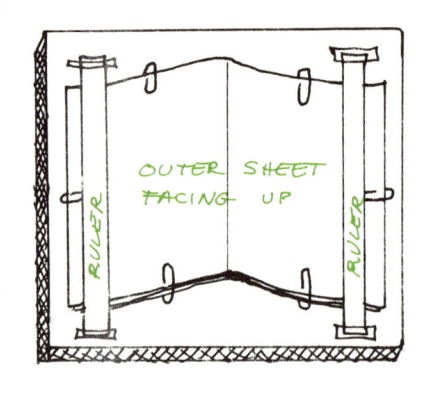

2. Follow directions in Chapter VI, Section E2, to make a 5-hole measuring guide ¾" wide and as tall as your page (10"). Line up the guide's *lengthwise* fold with the center fold of the top sheet. Place a bit of tape at the top and bottom ends of the guide to hold it onto the cardboard below; tape will leave a mark if it touches the page directly. Poke a pointed object such as a darning needle or nail into each hole and gently hammer it until the point pierces all pages and sticks into protective board below. Be sure pages do not slide out of line while you stab holes. When all holes are made, remove guide and make a lightly penciled number beside each hole on top sheet as shown. Remove rulers, but keep paper clips in place to hold pages together.

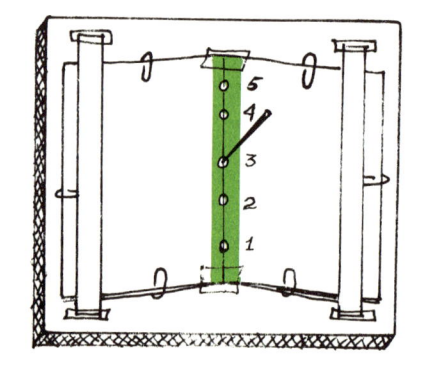

3. Cut a piece of button thread twice as long as book is high (2 times 10" = 20"). Pull thread through beeswax if you have it (see Chapter VI, Section D), to give it added strength. Thread darning needle and tie about 3" of one thread end into one paper clip.

4. Be sure all sheet edges are lined up, with holes directly under one another. Hold book in your hand and keep sheet with hole numbers facing you. Take the first stitch down into hole #1. The paper clip will catch against the paper and keep the thread from pulling through. Sew up into hole #2 from inside to outside. Turn book over if necessary to look at the position of holes on the other side. Sew down into hole #3 from outside. Sew up into #4, down into #5 as shown. Gently pull thread in direction of arrow so it will be taut (a). Then sew back down the row of holes. Sew up into #4 from inside, down into #3 from outside, up into #2 from inside. *Stop!* Pull thread taut once again. Remove paper clip from first thread end. On outside, tie thread ends together in a double knot (b). You may need a friend's finger to hold knot in place for you. Leave "tails" about ½" beyond knot, then cut off any extra thread. Remove paper clips from page edges. Use kneaded rubber or art gum eraser very delicately to erase numbers from sheet's center fold. Fold sheets in half again so that thread "tails" remain on outside of spine. If you have already decorated the outside sheet to make your cover, you can put a drop of rubber cement under the thread "tails" to hold them against the spine. Binding may be complete at this point, or the sewn signature may be used in the following more complex binding techniques.

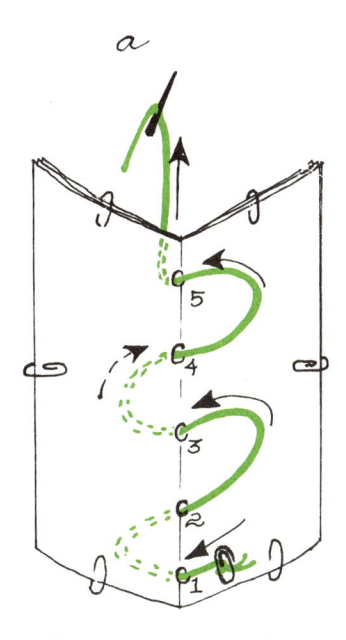

ENLARGED SKETCH SHOWING SEWING DIRECTION

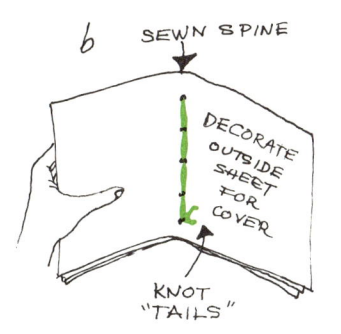

47

C. Single-Signature Book, Half-Bound

This method is used for books of up to 32 pages. For longer books, use a full-bound book with case, as in Section D of this chapter.

Materials: Page paper and cardboard for boards (see Chapter V), wax paper, decorative paper for board covers, cloth, Mystik tape in a color that goes well with the cover paper, rubber cement, ruler, utility knife, scissors, button thread, darning needle, beeswax (optional), mallet or wood block, pencil, paper clips, masking tape.

1. *Signature*. Fold and sew a single signature with up to 32 pages as described in Section B of this chapter but do *not* decorate the final sheet for a cover.

2. *Boards*. In this example, front and back covers will be made of paper-covered cardboard; the spine and corners of the board will be covered with colored cloth tape. (You may, instead, prefer to simplify the process by using an attractive precolored mat board, or cardboard *completely* covered with paper, and add the tape only to the spine; in this way you can omit the separately covered corners, step 8, and the cut paper cover, step 11.)

3. Make note of the size of one single book page (not the entire folded sheet). In example, page is 7½″ wide, 10″ high. Cut two boards each ⅛″ *less* wide than the page and ¼″ taller, or 7⅜″ by 10¼″. On the wrong side of each board, measure, mark, and draw dotted lines ⅛″ in from 3 edges as shown.

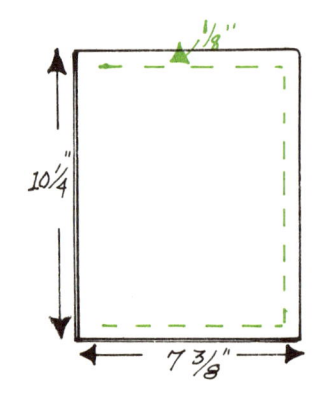

4. Place folded and sewn signature front side down on table. Pull knot "tails" of sewing thread over onto back sheet as shown and rubber-cement them down.

5. Brush rubber cement onto marked side of one cover board and onto back side of the signature's last sheet. Set glued signature and glued board beside each other as shown (a), with the board's unmarked edge facing the book's spine, and both head edges at the top. Carefully fold over the glued back sheet, pressing it down onto the board *in line with the dotted lines*. There should be an even ⅛″ margin of board around 3 edges of the page (b). Smooth page down onto board, pressing from center toward outer edges. There should be no wrinkles. Turn board over on top of signature and you will see that it is ¼″ away from the sewn spine. Repeat this step to glue the other half of the back sheet onto the *front* board. Note that as you will be working with the opposite, or *front*, side of the signature, positions in steps a and b will be reversed. The signature will be on the right, the board on the left, (c).

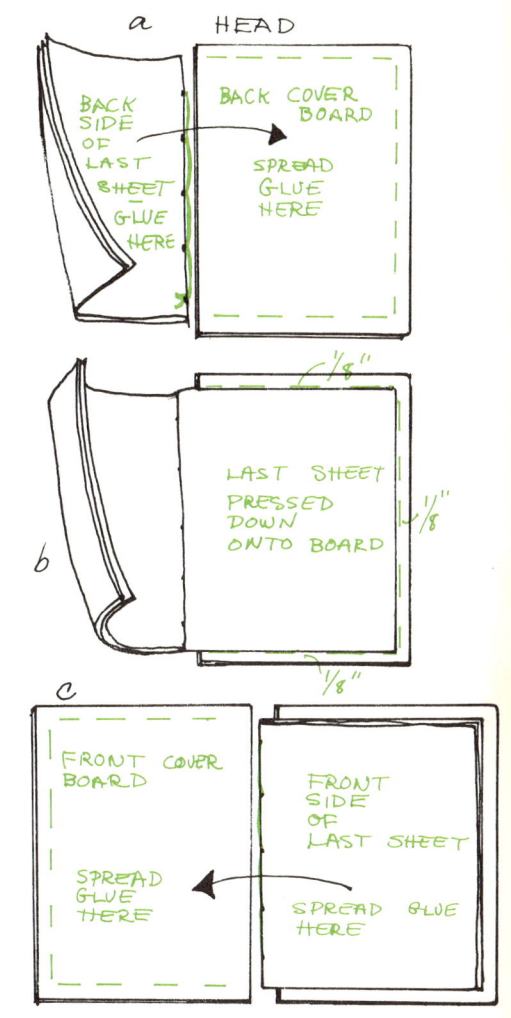

6. *Tape Spine Cover.* The following directions are for 1½″-wide cloth tape, which is quick and easy to use. This width tape is commonly available, but because it is quite narrow, it makes fairly small corners and requires 3 rows to cover the spine entirely. *Note*: Both spine and corners should be made of the same material; cloth or flexible paper may be substituted for the tape. If you do substitute, make the corners as large as you wish—considering the overall book design—and cut the spine covering 3″ wide and 1″ longer than height of cover board. Ignore steps 7 through 10 following, and rubber-cement spine cover to signature.

7. (a) On both front and back boards, measure, mark, and draw a light pencil line 1″ over from board's spine edge.

49

(b) Then place a ruler flat on the table. Tape will be measured on top of this ruler; it must be 1″ longer than the height of the cover board (10¼″ plus 1″ = 11¼″). Unroll tape slightly, press one end onto the beginning of the ruler, then unroll tape on top of ruler until you reach the 11¼″ mark. Cut tape off here. While tape is stuck to ruler, draw dotted lines in pencil or felt pen ½″ in from each end to mark the points where tape will fold over the cover boards.

(c) Carefully pull tape off ruler and stick one of its short ends onto the edge of a table so strip hangs freely and will not stick to itself. Keeping *sticky sides out*, fold the loose short end in half, pinching it tightly to mark the fold as shown.

(d) With scissors, make a short cut at fold mark on tape, then rip the 2 halves apart. Tape will tear easily in a straight line right down the center, making 2 strips, each ¾″ wide. Now stick both tape ends onto table as in step c until you are ready to work with them.

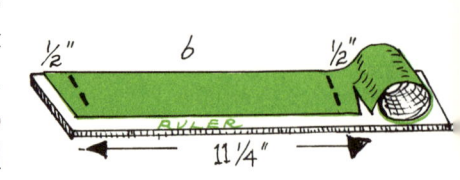

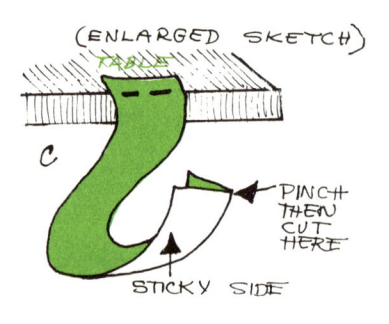

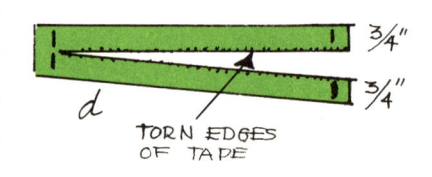

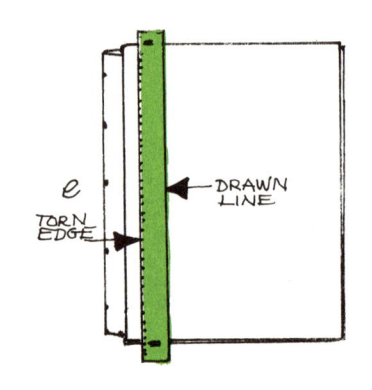

(e) Place the front board face up on the table. Remove one strip of tape from table edge. Hold both ends, and keep the torn edge to the left. Pull tape taut, and raise it, keeping torn edge to *left* of drawn line, just above board's surface, while you line up the *untorn* edge with line and arrange the ½″ margin marks so they extend evenly above and below board. When correctly lined up, press tape down and smooth flat. Fold over the ½″ tape margins and press them onto inside surfaces of board. Repeat on the *back* board, lining up *untorn* tape edge with drawn line and placing tape to the spine side of this line.

(f) Using the ruler as in step b, cut another strip of tape 11¼″ long. Cut 2 pieces of wax paper each 2½″ wide by ½″ long. Peel back each short end of tape. Center width of wax paper on tape's sticky side, pressing paper onto tape.

(g) Place book face up, spine to left. Lift this strip of tape from ruler. Hold the tape so one of its wax-paper strips extends ½″ beyond the head of the cover board as shown; overlap the right edge of the tape an even ⅛″ over the torn edge of the first tape strip and press it down. Smooth tape flat. At the foot edge, the bottom wax-paper strip should extend ½″. Press tape tight against left board edge and then flat out onto the paper spine. Do not allow tape to stick to table.

(h) Turn book over, with back board facing up. Pull the tape over and press it flat onto paper spine. Then press tape into the edge of the board and over onto the back board, overlapping the torn edge of the first tape about ⅛″ in an even line.

(i) Open book and turn over all pages so they lie flat on the right-hand board. Peel wax paper off top end of tape. Gently grasp tops of all pages (except glued-down back sheet) and—with one hand—pull them forward toward you and away from the boards while the other hand folds the tape over and down onto the boards and the back sheet that covers them. It may help to use an ice-cream stick or nail file to tuck in tape. Repeat with bottom end of tape.

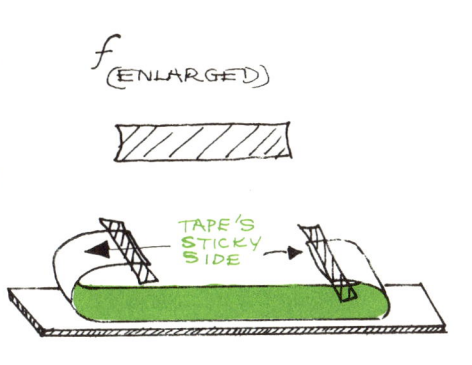

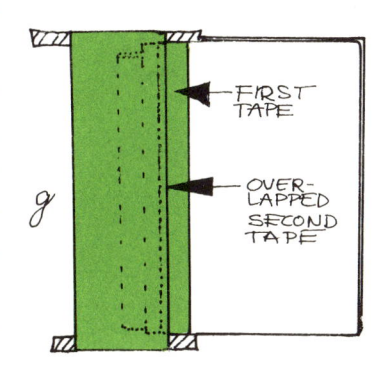

8. *Covered Corners.* (*Note*: In this example, we use tape corners to match the tape spine cover. If you prefer cloth or paper, make a paper pattern for the corner covers following directions below. Trace around pattern on cloth or paper, cut corners out, and rubber-cement them onto boards.) To begin, place book flat, front board up. With ruler and pencil, measure and mark dots at points X and Y, each 1¾" out from top fore-edge corner A. Mark dots at points X and Y, 1¾" out from bottom fore-edge corner B. Repeat this on outside surface of back board at corners C and D.

9. Cover one corner at a time. First, unroll a length of tape (roughly 5") and set it over marked corner as shown, lining up bottom tape edge with dots X and Y and allowing tape to overhang each side about ½" and the corner point about ¼" (arrow). Measure about ½" out from the board sides (dotted lines) and cut tape here (a). Press cut tape down against board edges as shown (b).

10. Open front board so its inside surface faces you and all pages remain on the right side. Grasp the tape overhang at the head edge, pull it firmly over, and press it down (a). Then make a small angled fold at the tip of the corner (b). Finally, pull the fore-edge overhang up and over, pressing it onto board to complete corner (c). Repeat on remaining corners, always folding up head or foot overhang first, then making corner angle, and *last* folding over fore-edge overhang.

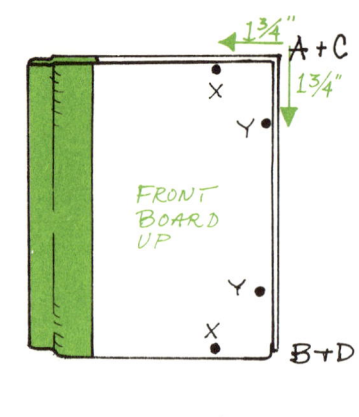

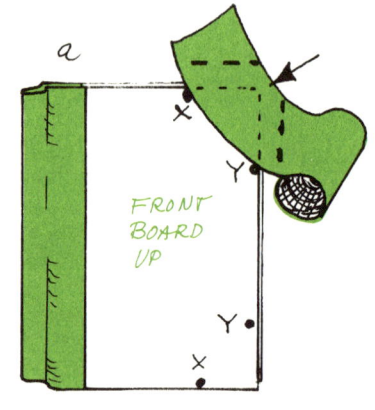

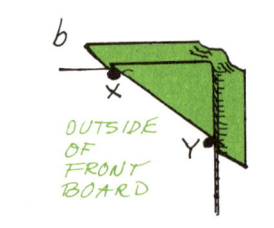

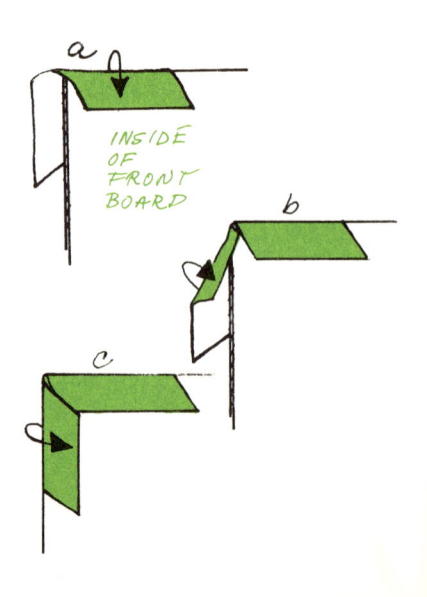

52

11. *Paper-Covered Boards.* (*Note*: This specially fitted cover paper is used primarily when corners and spine cover are made of cloth or paper with unevenly cut or unraveling edges. The paper should be neatly cut as it will overlap these edges about ⅛", giving the book a neat appearance. If you do not wish to cover the boards, see step 2 for alternatives.)

Open book and mark a light pencil X on the inside top of front board so you will always know which way is up while completing the binding.

(a) Make a measuring guide as follows. Cut a strip of scrap paper about 1½" wide and roughly 2" longer than book's *width*. In example, width is 7¾" plus 2" = 9¾".

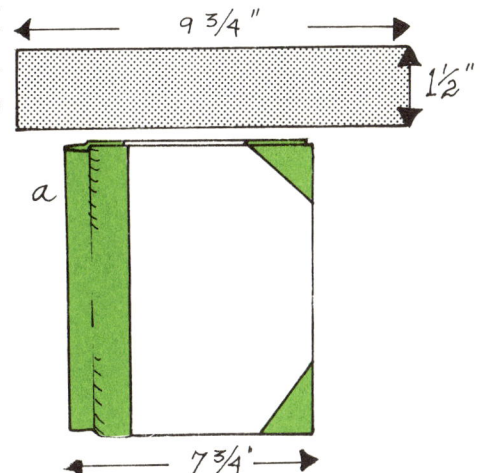

(b) Fold under about 1½" of one short end of the paper strip. Place book as shown, head up, spine to left. Tuck folded strip end inside front board about ⅛" below head edge. Paper-clip strip to edge to hold it in place.

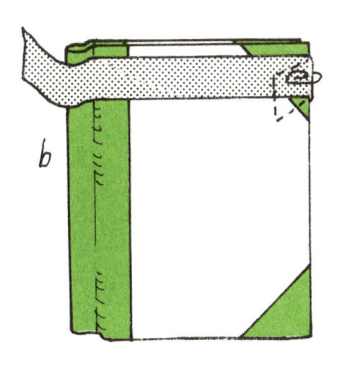

(c) Hold the measuring strip *parallel* to the head edge of book. Make a pencil mark on the strip where it folds over the fore-edge (point A). Then mark point B on strip *and on board* where strip overlaps the top covered corner about ⅛". Mark point C on strip and board where strip overlaps the spine cover about ⅛". Remove paper clips and flatten strip.

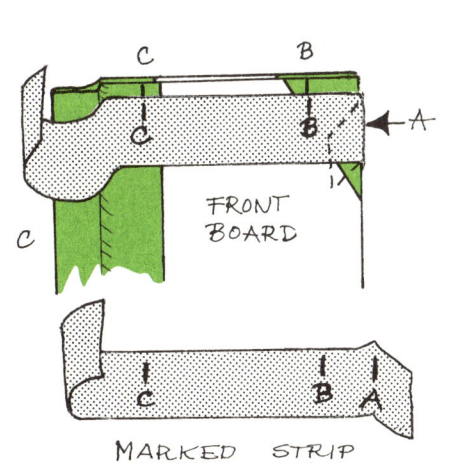

53

(d) Open book flat with both cover boards facing up, all pages underneath the back board as shown. Place measuring strip up against foot edge of front board. Line up point A exactly with tip of bottom corner. Holding strip in this position (tape it if necessary) make pencil dots on cover board at points corresponding to points B and C on strip. Then line up the strip along the fore-edge, place point A at the tip of *each* corner, and mark point B on second leg of *each* corner (arrows).

(e) Cut 2 cover papers, each the *same* width as a cover board (7⅜″) and 1″ more than board's height (10¼″ plus 1″ = 11¼″). Follow directions below for cutting front cover paper; this will later be used as a pattern for back cover paper. Place one paper flat on table, *right side up.* Measure and mark one dot, X, 1″ over from top left corner and ½″ down from head edge; mark dot, Y, 1″ over from bottom left corner and ½″ up from foot edge. Dots X and Y are your guide points indicating fold lines for later use in turning cover paper over onto boards.

(f) Close book and place it flat on table, front cover up, spine to left. Open front cover and slip in the cover paper marked side up. Slide paper to left until its left edge is exactly in line with spine cover points C *at both top and bottom.* Dots X and Y should line up evenly with head and foot edges of board, and paper should extend ½″ beyond head and foot edges all the way across the board. Press down on the front cover to hold paper in this position while making pencil dots on the

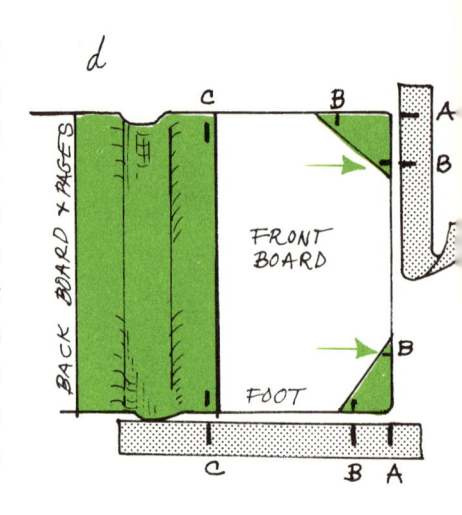

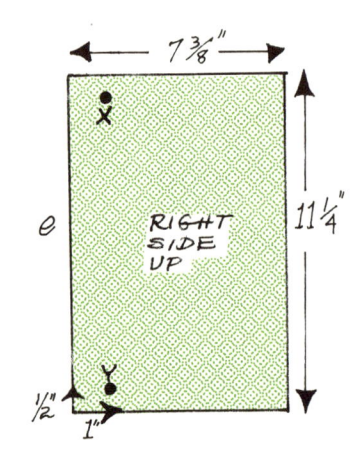

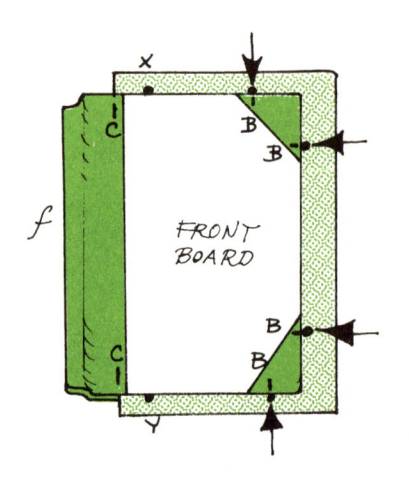

54

paper corresponding to points B on both legs of each corner (arrows).

(g) Remove paper from book, carefully keeping paper's head edge up. Turn paper face down and lightly pencil the word "head" on top of paper's wrong side. At fore-edge, fold back corners as shown, turning paper back until you see both corner dots B. Fold down a neat line joining dots at each corner (arrows, a). Cut along folds (b). Cover paper is now the correct size.

(h) Use this front cover paper as a pattern for the back, as follows. Set a large piece of cover paper flat, *right side up*. On top of it place the pattern piece, *wrong side up*. Tape papers flat onto table cover. Draw around the edge of the pattern, then cut along the lines.

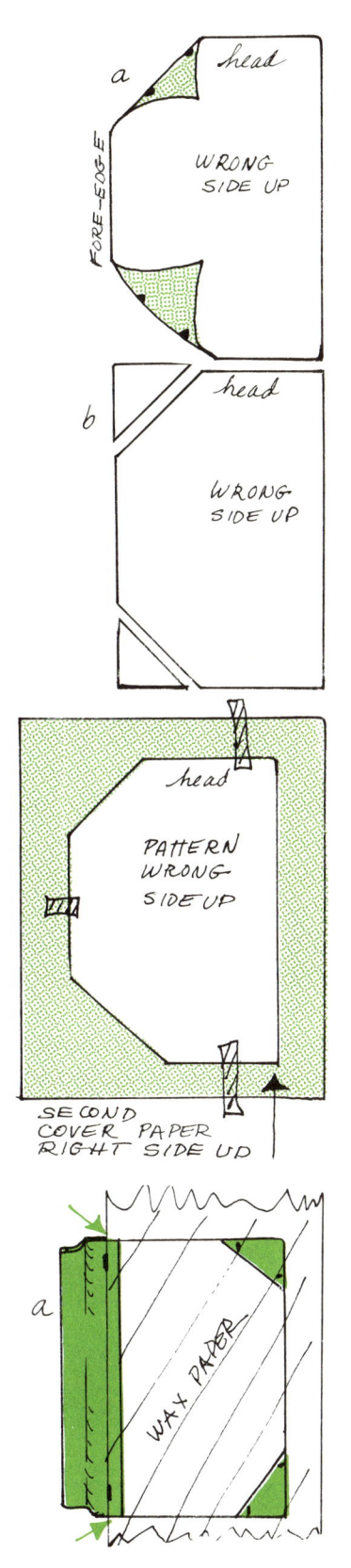

(i) If you plan to decorate cover papers, do it now before they are attached to the boards. To fasten paper to board, spread rubber cement over uncovered side of board, but only on a ⅛"-wide strip overlapping spine cover and corners. Remember, excess rubber cement rubs off. Also spread rubber cement all over *wrong side* of front cover paper; set this aside. Cut a long sheet of wax paper, place it on top of glued board as shown, with left edge just overlapping spine tape (arrows, a). Set cover paper, glued side down, on top of wax paper as shown (b). Slide cover paper into position so its left edge lines up with spine overlap at dots C and cut angles line up with corner dots B. Firmly hold down paper with one hand while with the other you slip out the wax paper (to the right side). Press cover paper down in place lightly by running your hand across center of paper from spine to fore-edge as shown. Do not let paper slide away from the marks. Cut a second piece of wax paper, place it over the cover paper, and smooth cover paper firmly down onto board, pressing from center out toward edges until there are no wrinkles.

(j) Open front cover, but leave all pages and endpaper facing toward the right side. Spread cement on the edges of the cover paper that are sticking out (x's). Also spread rubber cement all over back sheet on inside surface of front board (a). Pull overlap edges of cover paper tightly over board edges and press them down onto glued board. Spread rubber cement all over facing endpaper, Y. Turn endpaper over and lightly press it down onto glued board. Cover right surface of endpaper with another protective wax paper and press it down firmly, smoothing from center toward outside edges (arrows, b). Glued-down endpapers hide uneven tape and edges of cover paper, making a neat interior lining. Repeat steps h, i, j, to cover back board and attach back endpaper.

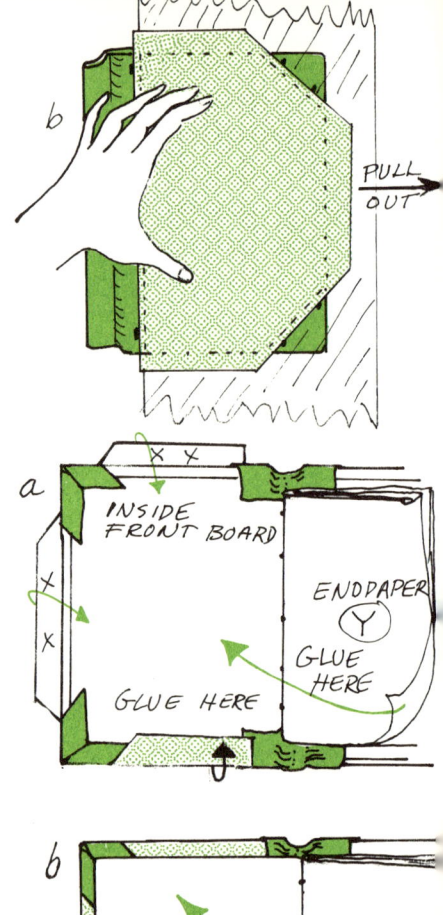

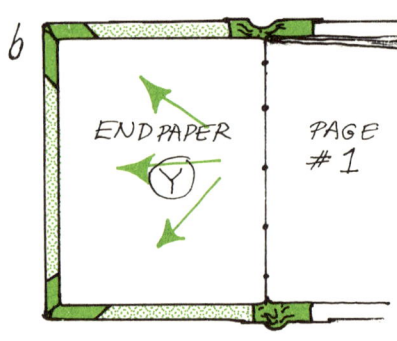

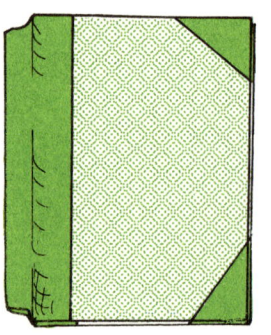

COMPLETE BINDING

56

D. Multi-Signature Book, Full-Bound with Case

This binding method is used for books with more than 32 pages, sewn in signatures. As in a library book, the signatures are bound to a covered, 3-sided cardboard case.

When you have more than 2 signatures (of 16 pages each) they should be sewn separately, then later fastened together, as described below. In this way the binding will be stronger and neater than if too many pages were sewn together into only 1 signature.

Materials: Page paper and cardboard for boards (see Chapter V), wax paper, decorative paper for board covers, rubber cement, masking tape, ruler, paper clips, darning needle, button thread, beeswax (optional), mallet or wood block, pencil, scissors, utility knife, large rubber bands.

1. Decide on your book's page size. Page *height* must be at least 9" in order to use sewing method described below. Page width should be in proportion to height. See Section B of this chapter for directions for folding and sewing signatures. Depending upon its length (see Chapter III, Sections A and B), your book will contain 2 or more signatures of 4 sheets (16 pages) each. If, when planning layout (Chapter III, Section C), you discover that your text will not completely fill the last signature, you may wish to revise your layout of the pages, dividing the extras and leaving half of them blank at the front of the book and half at the back; or, make one of the signatures with fewer than 4 sheets. *Note*: With this binding method, the first and last pages become the endpapers which are fastened to the boards; this takes a total of 4 sides (pages) away from text use.

Our example has 48 pages (4 will be endpapers) divided into 3 separately sewn signatures of 4 sheets (16 pages) each. Single page size is 7½" wide, 10" high; unfolded *sheet* size is 15" wide, 10" high.

2. To make signatures, follow directions in Section B of this chapter; in *steps 1, 2, and 3* make the *following changes* to mark, poke through, and number signature holes. Do *not* sew into them.

Change 1: In step 1, do not add 2 extra sheets for back sheet and endpapers.

Change 2: In step 3, after numbering holes on top sheet, turn entire stack of pages over, so center fold is facing up. Keep stack's head edge up, so hole #5 is still at top (look underneath to be sure). *Lightly* (so it can later be erased) pencil hole numbers along the fold facing you as shown.

3. *Sewing.* Before sewing the signatures to each other, sew each separately, BUT ONLY BETWEEN HOLES #1 AND #2, AND #4 AND #5. To do this, first cut thread about 12″ long and tie one end around a paper clip. Keeping signature opened as in step 2 above, paper-clip edges of all sheets together so pages will stay lined up evenly while being handled. Then turn stack over, center fold down, so that the last sheet faces up, and hole #5 is at the top. Holding the signature in this position with one hand, take the first stitch down into hole #5. Paper clip will catch on spine and keep thread from pulling through. Bring thread across inside fold and back out hole #4 (a). Place signature flat on table, remove paper clip, pull threads taut, and tie them into a double knot tight against spine (ask a friend to help hold knot flat as you tie it). Cut off thread ends about ¼″ beyond knot. Repeat, sewing through holes #1 and #2 in the same way (b). Do this on each signature.

4. To sew signatures together, cut thread twice as long as page height (2 times 10″ = 20″). Run thread through beeswax if you have it (see Chapter VI, Section D). Thread needle, tie about 3″ of one thread end onto a paper clip. Set 2 signatures side by side with spines touching, fore-edges facing away from each other (a).

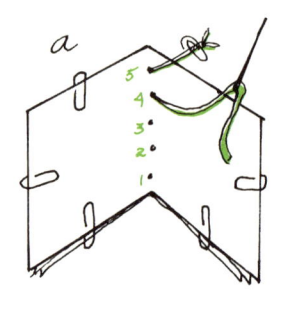

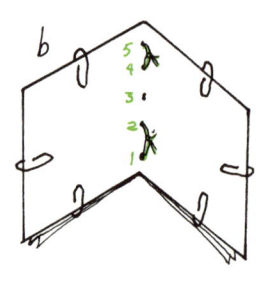

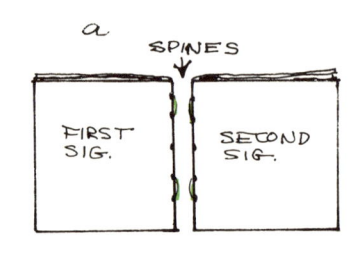

58

Line up head and foot edges, then open each signature to its center. Place the top halves of each signature back to back and paper-clip them together at arrows (b).

5. Holding the first 2 signatures in position shown, stitch from hole #1 in first signature through hole #1 in second, then back toward left, through both holes #2 to the inside of first signature (a). Paper clip will catch on fold and keep thread from pulling through. Then follow diagram (b), stitching into holes #3, back toward left through #4, into #5 to the right. Pull thread taut, then follow diagram (c) to stitch back down the line, sewing into holes #4, #3, and #2 from alternate sides. *Stop!* Pull thread taut. Now turn center group of pages over toward the right, closing second signature, and flattening the right-hand page, X, of first signature. Untie thread end from paper clip. Keeping threads tight against fold, tie ends into a double knot. Cut thread ends off about ¼" beyond the knot.

6. Signatures #1 and #2 are now sewn together. Place them flat, with second signature on top and spines to the *right*. Place third signature (if you have one) beside them, spines touching as shown. Line up head and foot edges. Open second and third signatures to their centers. Place top half of each signature back to back and paper-clip them together as in step 4, (b). To sew signatures together, prepare another thread as in step 4. Follow sewing directions as in steps 4 and 5 above. More

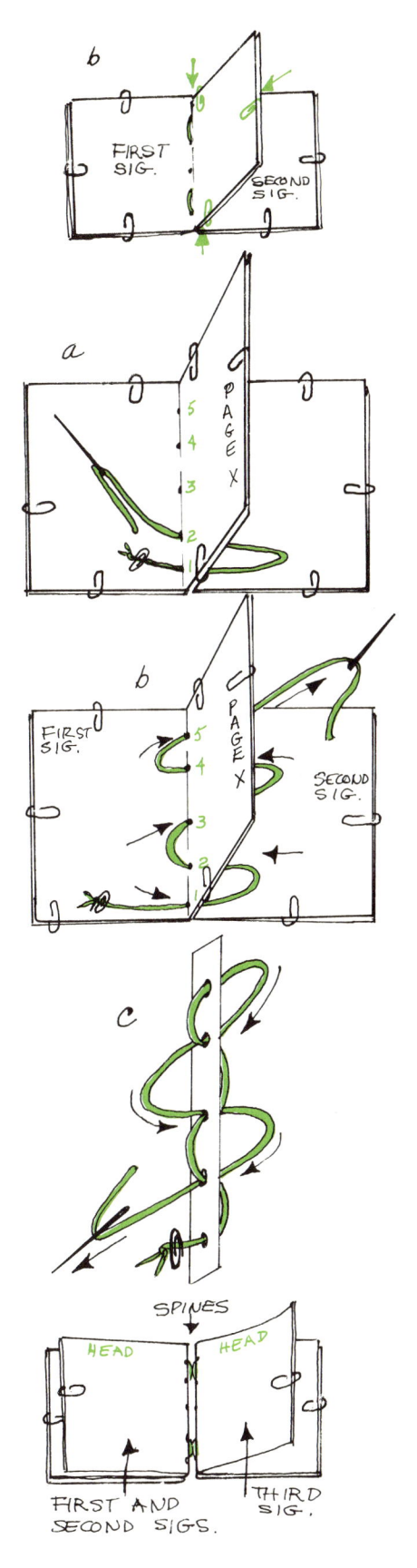

59

signatures may be added in the same manner. When sewing is complete, remove all paper clips.

7. *Tapes.* Binding tapes are wide pieces of paper (or stiff cloth) slipped beneath the *outside* spine threads which you see between holes #1 and #2 and #4 and #5. Tapes are glued down onto the boards to help reinforce the binding.

To make the tapes, cut 2 pieces of medium-weight paper (or cotton or linen cloth) each 1¾" by 4½". Bring short ends together to fold each tape in half crosswise (a). Set sewn book flat, spine sticking out slightly beyond table edge as shown (b). Slip a darning needle beneath the threads between holes #1 and #2. *Gently* pry theads out a little from spine; at the same time slip one tape's short end down behind needle (c). Pull tape down until threads are centered on tape's fold. Remove needle. Repeat, placing second tape beneath threads between spine holes #4 and #5.

8. *Mull.* A mull is a piece of paper or stiff cloth glued to the tapes and spine and then glued to the boards. It helps make the binding strong. Most library books, which have particularly durable bindings, are bound with tapes and a mull.

Make your mull of the same material used for the tapes in step 7. First, measure the distance between holes #1 and #5 along the spine (8" in our example). Cut mull this length (8") by 4½" wide. Fold mull in half lengthwise as shown.

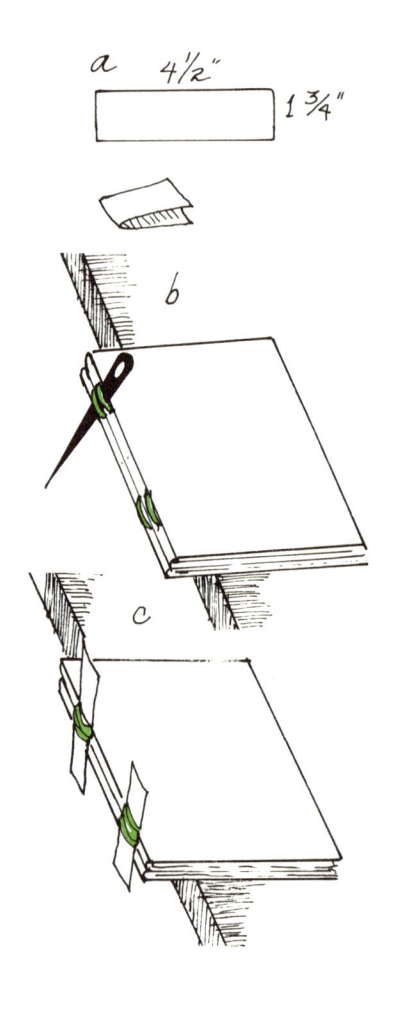

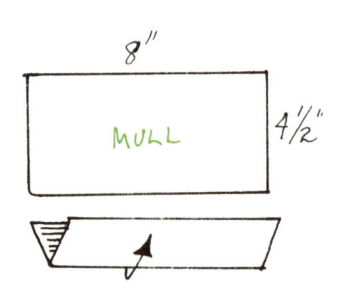

9. To attach mull to tapes, first place book in same position shown in step 7, (b), with spine extending slightly past the table edge. Cut a piece of scrap paper to roughly page size. Set it over the top endpaper, then fasten the top half of each binding tape onto the scrap paper with a bit of masking tape. Spread rubber cement on top half of each binding tape (X's) and all along spine, between holes #1 and #5, and over the tapes (colored area).

10. Spread rubber cement all over inside surface of mull (a). With glued surface facing down, press center fold of mull onto glued spine of book, lining up mull ends exactly with holes #1 and #5. Press top half of mull flat onto glued binding tapes (b). Remove masking tape and lift binding tapes from scrap paper. If pieces of masking tape should be sandwiched beneath the mull just cut off the exposed ends. Turn book over. Cover top sheet with scrap paper and repeat this step to glue the other half of the mull onto back halves of binding tapes. Then, with your forefinger, press mull firmly in against glued spine.

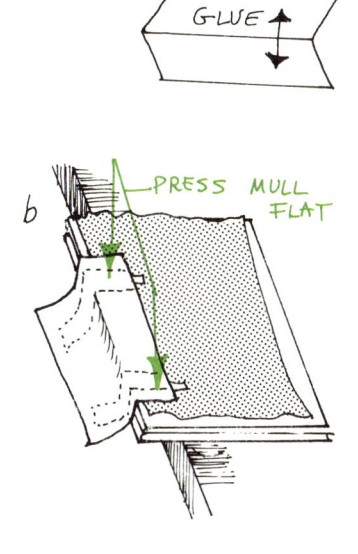

11. *Case.* The case is made of stiff front, back, and spine boards all covered with paper (as in example) or cloth. Choose illustration or mat board (see Chapter V) to make the case, and cover it with a strong, durable, flexible paper or cloth. Test a scrap of cover material to be sure it will not crack when folded or soil easily when handled. The case is made slightly larger than the actual page size in order to protect the pages.

12. Tape 2 scrap pieces of your cover board together side by side to give you a handy 2-board-thick measuring guide. Set this aside; it will be used for marking the binding at various stages.

13. To determine the size of front and back boards, place book flat as shown, spine to left. Top sheet is the endpaper. Hold 2-board measuring guide (step 12) up against the head edge at spine as shown, and mark point A on endpaper. Mark will be 2 boards' thickness out from spine (roughly between 1/8" and 3/16"). Use ruler to measure from point A to top fore-edge corner, point B (7⅜" in example). To this, add ⅛" for protective overhang at fore-edge; total board width is thus 7⅜" plus ⅛", or 7½". Board height is the height of the signature (10") plus ⅛" overhang at head and ⅛" at foot (10" plus ⅛" plus ⅛" = 10¼"). Cut 2 boards 10¼" by 7½".

14. Place book between front and back boards with mull flaps folded in against the endpapers. Stretch a large rubber band around the book's width to hold boards and book together. Slide the boards over to line up exactly with *spine* edge.

15. To measure the width of your spine board, you must know thickness of the spine plus the front and back boards. Wrap a piece of scrap paper around spine of book as shown, and pinch it tightly in order to mark the points (arrows) where it folds over board edges (a). Unwrap and

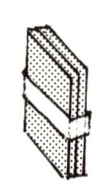

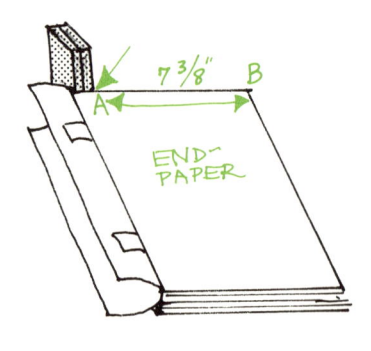

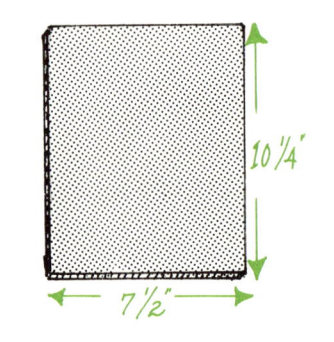

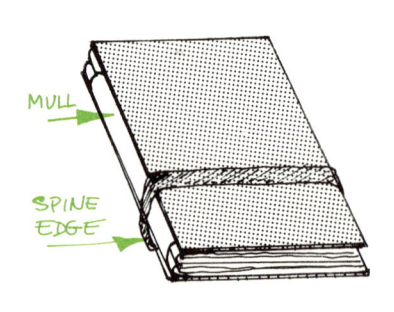

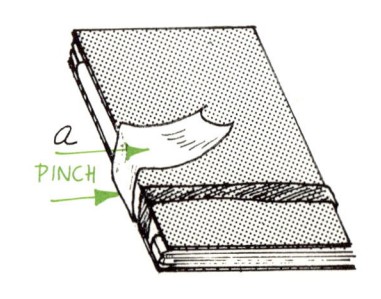

flatten strip, and measure distance between pinched marks (b). In example, the distance is ⅜". Cut one spine cardboard ⅜" wide by same height as front and back boards (see step 13; 10¼").

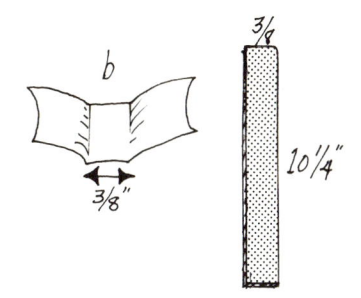

16. *Cover Paper.* The cardboard case is decorated with cover paper, a single sheet which wraps around and is glued to the front, spine, and back boards. On either side of the spine board there is a narrow, flexible "hinge" or strip of cover paper *without* any cardboard beneath it; this hinge allows covers to open easily.

To measure the width of the cover paper, add the width of front board (7½") plus width of spine (⅜") plus width of back board (7½") plus 2" for turnover; total is 17⅜". (*Note*: If your spine is more than ½" thick, allow 3" or more for turnover when planning these dimensions.) Height of cover paper is height of board (10¼") plus 1½" turnover; total = 11¾". Cut paper 17⅜" by 11¾".

17. Set cover paper flat, *wrong side up.* If right side of paper has a decorative pattern on it, be sure the top of the pattern is at the head edge. *Note*: To begin, you will work with the right end of the paper, covering the *back* board. It may help to weight down the left end of the paper so it does not curl up. Measure, mark, and draw dotted lines A, B, and C each ¾" in from head, foot, and right fore-edge (a).

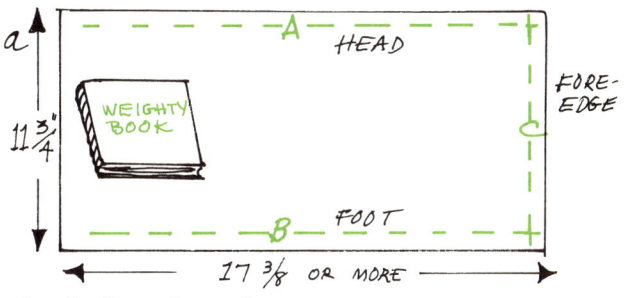

Then set down back board with its head and foot edges in line with dotted lines A and B, its right edge against line C. Hold board down, and draw line D along left edge of board (b). Lift board, spread rubber cement on its wrong side and on the paper in the board's area. Press board into place on the paper.

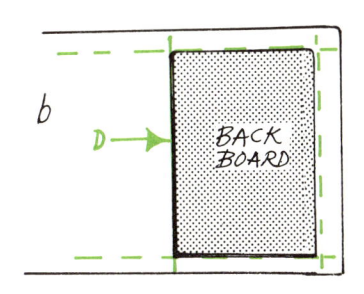

63

18. To mark a hinge strip between back board and spine, take the 2-board measure you made in step 12, hold one side of it tightly up against line D (left edge of back board) and mark its thickness. Repeat, marking 2-board thickness all along line D. Use ruler to connect these marks, drawing line E *parallel* to line D (line must not slant).

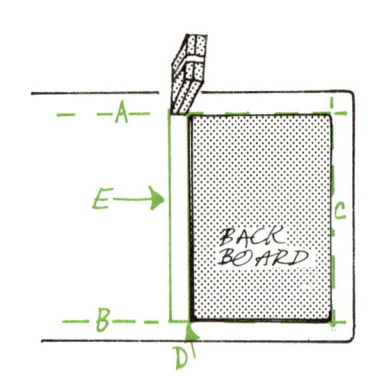

19. To attach the spine board, spread rubber cement on cover paper in a ⅜" to ½" wide strip just to the left of line E, between dotted lines A and B. Also spread cement on wrong side of spine board. With short ends of glued spine board touching lines A and B, and one long edge on E, press it onto glued paper.

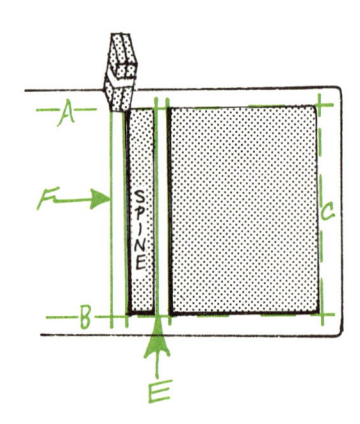

20. To mark a hinge strip on the other side of the spine, hold the 2-board measure tightly against left spine edge, mark its thickness, then draw line F between marked points.

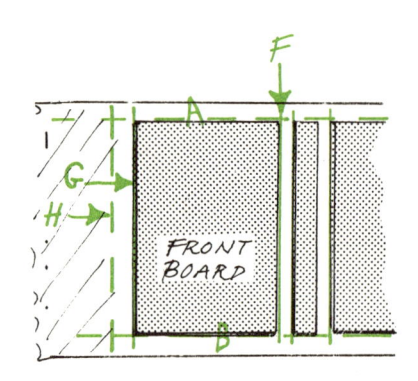

21. Place front board on the cover paper up against line F, with head and foot edges against dotted lines A and B. Hold board in this position and draw line G along its left edge. Lift board. Measure, mark, and draw dotted line H, ¾" to left of line G. (This may or may not work out to be the left edge of cover paper—depending on how wide your hinge strips are.) Cut off any paper extending beyond line H. Glue front board in place on proper area in the same manner you glued on back board and spine.

22. To make neatly turned-over corners, an angle is cut off each corner of the cover paper. First, mark the *outside* corners of front and back boards with the thickness of the 2-board measure (arrow). At marked points, draw angled lines as shown. Cut on lines, and remove the 4 corners.

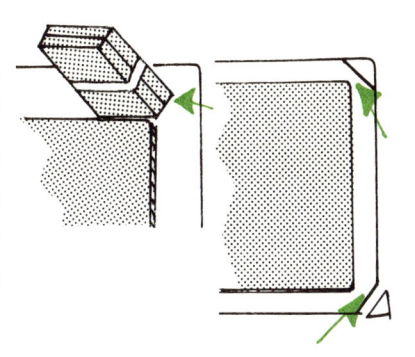

23. Spread rubber cement on all the edges of cover paper which stick out beyond the boards. Also spread a ¾"-wide strip of rubber cement on the head, foot, and fore-edges of front and back boards and on the head and foot edges of spine board (X's, a). Follow directions in Section A, step 5 of this chapter to turn over and glue down paper flaps (b).

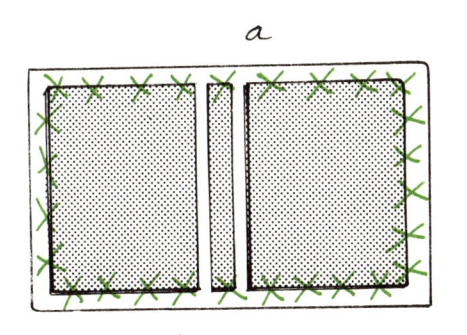

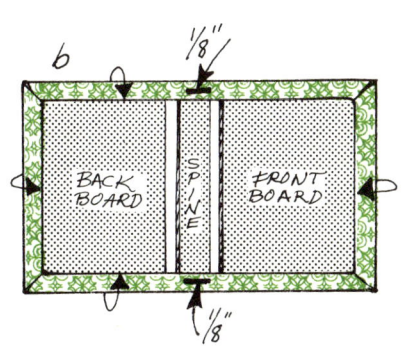

24. At head and foot edges of spine board, measure and mark points ⅛" in from outer edges (see b above).

25. Spread rubber cement along the length of the spine board between these 2 marks. Spread rubber cement all along spine of sewn book (X's, c), and over outside of mull as well. Holding book closed, with its head edge facing head edge of case, line up its spine between the ⅛"

marks on spine board. Positioning the book here is critical. Its spine must line up along *center* of spine board or book will be on a slant inside the case. Press glued spines together (a). To attach spine more firmly to case, hold sides of case together and stand book up on its foot as shown (b). Push gently in against fore-edge pages (colored arrows), then run a forefinger firmly along outside of case spine.

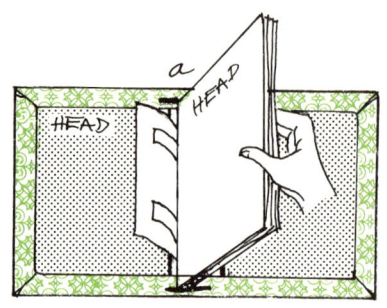

26. Close book and set it on table with front cover up. Open cover as shown and gently, with a bouncing motion, push down on front fore-edge until you see a narrow folded hinge appear alongside the spine.

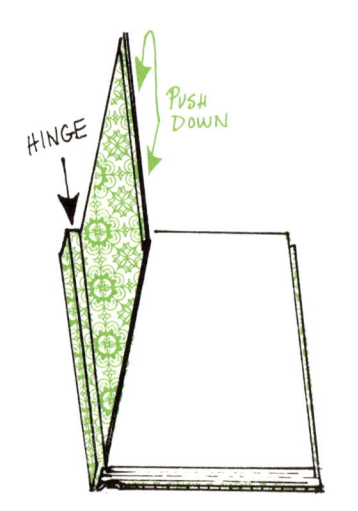

27. With front cover opened, turn mull over onto it; fold mull down so it rests flat on front board. Rubber-cement the mull firmly in place in this position. Use plenty of cement and be sure mull is well attached in order to have a strong binding. Repeat steps 26 and 27 on back side of book, pressing the hinge and gluing down the mull.

28. To complete binding, endpapers will now be attached to the inside of front and back boards. First set book in the position shown, with front cover opened. Slip a piece of wax paper under the top endpaper to protect pages from rubber cement. Spread rubber cement all over surface of endpaper and all over inside of front board (X's).

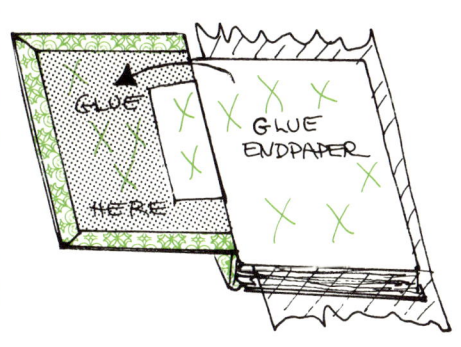

29. Hold the back board and all pages up at right angle to table as shown; turn over glued endpaper and press it down flat onto board. An even 1/8" border should show all around 3 sides of the endpaper (because cover is 1/8" larger than page).

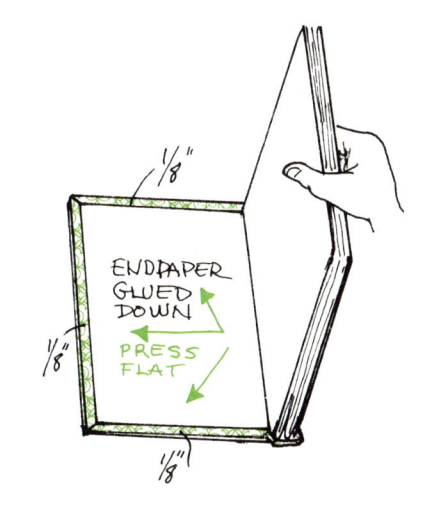

30. Now set back cover and pages flat on the table. Cover glued endpaper with protective wax paper and press it flat, working from center out toward edges. Repeat steps 28, 29, and 30 to attach back endpaper. Binding is now complete; to make a dust jacket, see Chapter IX, Section B.

IX. THE DUST JACKET

A. Purposes

The original purpose of the dust jacket was strictly to protect the book. Now the jacket is also a decorative part of the binding. Originally, jackets were of plain paper, often with holes or windows cut in them so one could read the title printed on the board underneath. Modern techniques of rapid, large-quantity printing as well as the popularity of advertising and promotion have led to the creation of the modern dust jacket: a wraparound, eye-catching poster which provides the potential reader with an instant summary of basic information about the book.

The dust jacket has five parts: the front and back covers, the spine, and two folded-over flaps which hold it onto the book. The front cover sometimes has a design on it which is related to the book's theme; it also tells the book's title, the name of the author or editor and/or illustrator, and publisher. The spine tells the title, author's name, and publisher so this information can be read even when the book is standing on a shelf. The back cover may have a design related to that on the front, or it may carry printed material such as reviews of this or other books, a *blurb* (see below), or biographical information about the author or illustrator. In the early history of printed dust jackets, the inside surface of the jacket was sometimes printed with all sorts of advertisements, which did not necessarily have anything to do with books; for example, soap, household items, stoves, coal. The front flap traditionally contains the *blurb*, a brief description of the book's contents. The blurb is intended to capture the reader's interest but not tell the entire story. The back flap usually tells you about the author and/or illustrator. You will, of course, find many variations in this pattern. Because dust jackets tend to tear and look worn after books are handled in shipping and in stores, some books, such as the one you are now reading, do not have separate jackets at all; instead, the cover paper is made of especially durable material and printed with the traditional jacket information. Flap copy appears elsewhere within the book. When planning your dust jacket you may follow the format outlined here, or design your own to suit the needs of your book.

Materials: When selecting paper for your jacket, remember that it must fold easily without cracking and be durable in order to survive handling. Very thin or slippery paper is not suitable. Art papers (vellum, charcoal paper, bond, etc.), some wallpapers, or strong gift-wrapping papers work well (see Chapter V). Other materials: ruler, scissors, pencil, scrap paper, masking tape, paper clips.

B. How to Make It

1. Select paper for your dust jacket. If it has a decorative pattern on it, you may want to design a solid-colored title label to be rubber-cemented in place on the front cover (and perhaps the spine as well). Solid-colored paper may be decorated with your own designs (see Chapter III, Section G).

2. To accurately measure the size of your jacket paper, cut a strip of scrap paper 2″ wide and *four* times as long as the *width* of your book's cover board. (This will give you some extra length to work with.) For example, if your board is 7½″ wide, the strip should be 30″ long (a). We will call the left short edge of this strip point A. Measure and mark point B, 4″ to the right of point A (b). (*Note*: Area A–B is for one of the folded jacket flaps. If you have a very large book, these flaps may be made 4½″ or wider; for a very small book the flaps may be narrower.) Fold strip over at point B. Paper-clip this folded end (point A to the inside) onto the back cover board of the book. Wrap remaining strip around the book as shown (c). Be sure strip goes straight around and is not on a slant. Close book with strip on it and be sure strip fits; it should be neither too tight nor too loose and book should open and close easily.

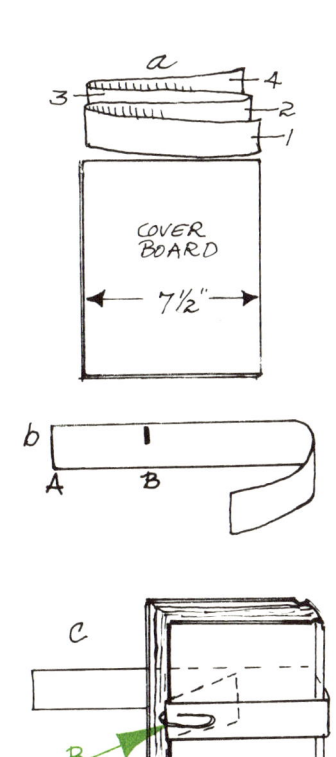

Now fold remaining strip end around onto the inside of front cover board. Paperclip the end in place and mark this fold at point C, as shown. Again check to be sure strip is parallel to head and foot of book. Pinch strip onto edges of spine.

3. Remove strip from book and press it out flat, marked side up. Measure and mark point D, 4″ to the right of point C. (*Note:* Distance C–D should equal A–B). Cut strip *straight* off at point D. The strip is now the correct length for your jacket paper.

4. Measure the length of the strip. In example, 24″. Cut (see Chapter VI, Section A) the jacket paper this width (24″) by the *same height* as your book's cover board (10¼″ in example). Set jacket paper, right side up, flat on table; tape corners down very lightly (so tape does not mar finish of paper). Tape down strip, marked side up, against bottom long edge of jacket paper, with left strip edge A evenly lined up with jacket paper's left edge. Carefully mark a light pencil dot on jacket paper in line with points B and C. Point D should be even with paper's right edge. Then untape strip and set it along the *top* long edge of the jacket paper. Tape strip down, in exactly the same position as before, with point A over left top edge. Again mark points B and C on jacket.

5. Untape jacket paper. Turn it *wrong side up* and make a fold connecting both marked points B as shown. This is the jacket's back flap.

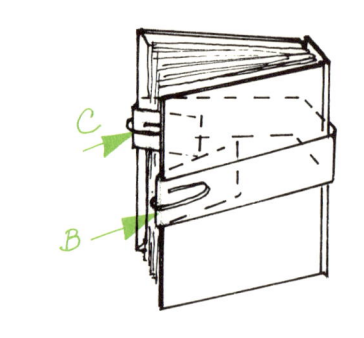

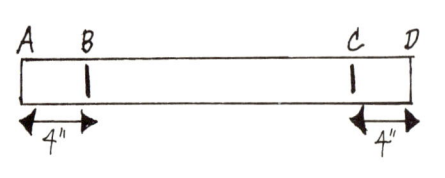

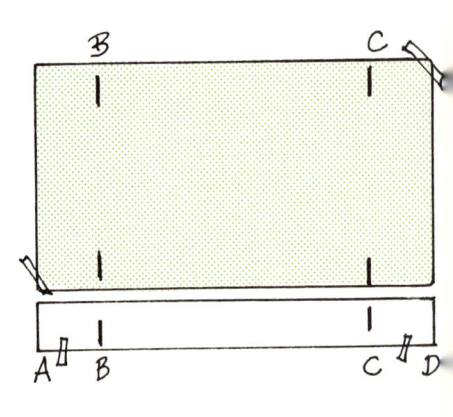

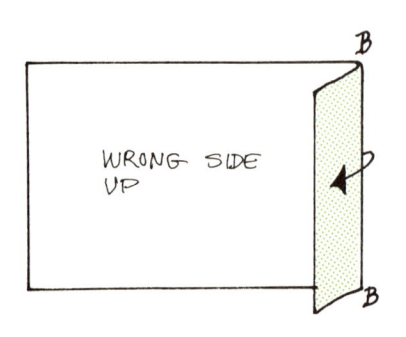

6. Tuck this flap inside the back board of the book and wrap the jacket (right side out) around your book as you did with the paper strip in step 2. Smooth the jacket tightly against the book, pulling it taut while holding the back flap in place. Pinch the jacket in against the spine edges, then fold the front flap onto the inside of the front board at points C. The jacket should fit around the book easily, as strip did in step 2. Remove the jacket from the book and press carefully along each fold marked during the fitting.

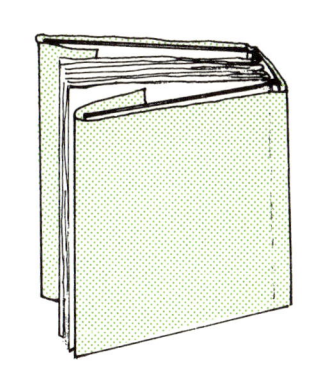

7. The jacket may now be completed by spreading it out flat and decorating the front, back, and flap areas as you wish. When decorations are dry, wrap the dust jacket around the book. Your book is now complete.

X. LET'S LOOK AT A PRINTED BOOK

A. What Does It Look Like?

Now that you have had the experience of making your own book, you will find that you can discover a lot just by looking at a printed book. Pick up any hard-cover book, and examine it as if you had never seen a book before. What is the first thing you notice? Its size, shape, thickness, weight, or color? Look at the way the book is held together—the binding. Are the front and back boards stiff? Thick or thin? Is the spine covered by a board? Are the boards covered with cloth or paper? Is the book quarter-, half-, or full-bound? What information is printed on the dust jacket, if there is one? Is there anything printed on the front cover? Look at the inside surfaces of the front and back boards. Can you see where the cover material was turned over the edges of the boards and glued down? Are the endpapers printed or plain, colored or white? Look down inside the spine. Can you see where the pages are folded, gathered into signatures, and sewn together? Can you tell how many signatures were used? Open the book to the center page of one of the signatures. Can you see the threads running along the fold? Can you tell how many holes were made for the sewing?

If you look closely at a *paperback* book, you will usually find that it is made of all single sheets held together at the spine with glue. This is called a *perfect binding*. Sometimes there is a paper or linen strip over the glue. The best quality paperback books are made of folded, sewn signatures glued together at the spine and between adjoining signatures.

B. What Can You Learn from the Pages?

Before the text or story of a book begins, there are always several pages of information called *front matter*. Additional material following the text is called *back matter*. Front and back matter together are sometimes called *oddments*, an appropriate name for these assorted bits of information. The order of the oddments may vary with each book, but certain basic information is always given, as you will see later on in this chapter.

As you look through a book, you will see that most of the time the important pages or sections begin on a right-hand page—a custom stemming from the ancient folk belief that the right side is superior, the place of honor. Placement and order vary with different cultures.

Because the Hebrew language is written from right to left, books in Hebrew are held with the spine toward the *right* side; compared to English books, it looks like they read from back to front. Frequently Oriental books are read with the spine held at the right, and both Chinese and Japanese writing may be set either in vertical columns or horizontal lines.

Between the front cover and the first printed page there may be one or several blank or illustrated pages. The first right-hand page with type we will refer to as page 1, but these page numbers are for convenience only since they may or may not be the same as the numbers in your book. Page 1 contains only the title, but is called a *half-title* because it tells you only the book's title and nothing more. It is believed that the use of a half-title dates from the time when the earliest printed books were shipped to the bindery in unbound bundles. As handling soiled it, the top page was at first left blank. But the binder needed some identification of what was inside, so a half-title was added, with the real title page, giving the full information, kept clean and protected underneath. Page 2, the reverse side of the half-title, may be blank, or may list previous books by the same author. The *title page* may either be a "double-page spread," covering pages 2 and 3, or stand alone on page 3. The title page tells the book's full title, and subtitle if there is one. It also tells the name of the author(s), the illustrator(s), editor(s), or translator(s), and the name and location of the publisher. (If you want to write to a publisher about a book, you can locate him by using this information as a starting point and consulting a telephone book for the specific address.)

The reverse of the title page, page 4, tells you about the *copyright*, a legal right guaranteeing that the holder will be the only one to produce and sell the work. If someone else then produces and sells the work without permission, legal action can be taken against him. Copyrights last for a specific number of years and may then be renewed. If the copyright is not renewed, the material will pass into the "public domain" where *anyone* may produce and sell it without permission or payment to the author or publisher. The copyright is indicated by an international symbol ©. It is followed by the name of the person or persons holding the copyright (author or publisher, etc.) and the date it takes effect, which is the year the book is first published. You will not need a copyright for your book; a copyright can be obtained only when a book is published.

Near the copyright, you may also see a statement that "all rights are reserved" or something similar—a legal phrase that means the property rights belong to the author or publisher and no one else can copy or resell or otherwise use the work without permission and/or payment.

Copyright © 1973 by Susan Purdy
All rights reserved
Printed in the United States of America
First Edition

There may also be a statement telling the country in which the book was printed, and the number assigned the book by the Library of Congress in Washington, D.C., which has a record of all books published in the U.S.A. Usually you will see a note identifying the edition or number of printings, and less often, the name of the typographer or designer who selected and planned the book's type.

The next right-hand page, page 5, may be the *dedication*. Originally, the dedication was a long and flowery statement in which the author symbolically gave the book to someone important—his king or queen, a patron who supported him, or his friend. Today, dedications are usually fairly short and are made to friends or family or a group about whom the author cares particularly. Some authors omit the dedication entirely.

Page 6 may be blank, illustrated, or contain an *epigraph*, a quotation the author feels is related to the meaning of the book. Page 7 may contain *acknowledgments*, the author's thanks to others who have helped him. Pages 6 and 7 might also be the *table of contents*, or this might appear on a single, right-hand page, 9. This is a guide to the use of the book, and generally lists all chapters or sections and the pages on which they begin. If there are many photographs, drawings, charts, or maps, you may find them listed on the right-hand page immediately following the table of contents.

Also following the table of contents, you may find an explanation of the book, its purpose or background. Usually, if this is written by the author, it is called a *preface*; if it is written by someone else, it is called a *foreword*. This may be followed or replaced by an *introduction* explaining the book's purpose or method of use.

The front matter is followed by the body, text, of the book. This usually begins on a right-hand page whether or not it is divided into chapters or sections.

At the end of the text, you find back matter, which is any reference material, such as an *appendix* (supplementary information), *glossary* (list of definitions), *bibliography* (list of reference works), *index* (detailed guide to contents by subject and page), *colophon* (list of details about a book's design: designer's name, name of printer and binder, type of paper, name of type face, etc.), and author's and illustrator's biographical information. Back matter is often found in books of nonfiction, but rarely in fiction. The *dust jacket*, explained more fully in Chapter IX, was originally meant to protect the book. It is now used primarily as advertisement telling you briefly about the book and its author and illustrator. Great effort goes into making the jacket as attractive as possible—to make the book something you want to pick up, examine, and possibly buy.

XI. HOW ARE PRINTED BOOKS MADE?

Printed books are physically produced by a publisher. The process of book publishing, at first glance, may seem enormously complicated, but professionally published books are written, illustrated, and bound in much the same way you did your own following the directions in this book. Thus you will already be familiar with many of the procedures that follow. References to methods you have used will be given in parentheses. The most important elements at each stage of production will be italicized to set them apart.

A. What Is the First Step?

As you know from trying to write your own book, an author cannot begin until he or she has an *idea*. A book idea may originate with the author or it may be suggested by the publisher. Each author works out ideas in a different manner, and there are no set rules, but eventually every author makes a first draft as you did in Chapter I, Section C, which may be handwritten, typed, or spoken into a tape recorder. Usually the first draft will need to be revised, corrected, perhaps reorganized, and finally retyped to make the final manuscript. In some cases, the material may be rewritten two, three, or even a dozen times, until the author is satisfied with the result.

B. How Does a Book Get Published?

To turn a final manuscript into a printed book, the author needs to find a publisher. Authors may mail the manuscript—with or without accompanying illustrations—directly to a publisher, or use a literary agent, a specialist who places written material with publishers and handles resulting business matters.

A publishing house employs people to select manuscripts and produce books from them. They try to select manuscripts which they believe several thousand people will enjoy and want to buy. Still other employees distribute, advertise, and sell these books.

More than a thousand manuscripts may be submitted to a publishing house during a year, but in most cases fewer than a hundred of these will be published. An individual in a publisher's office, called a *reader*, reads all manuscripts that come in. Some are sent back to the author with a notice of rejection because the reader, experienced in the kind of material in which the publisher is likely to be interested, knows it to be unsuitable. Because of the large number of manuscripts submitted, it may take anywhere from six to eight weeks or more for a publisher to respond to an "unsolicited" (unrequested) manuscript. Some manuscripts the reader will send on to an editor or other members of the firm for further reading and consideration. Some of these will be rejected, too, but some will be accepted for publication.

C. What Exactly Does the Publisher Do?

When a book is accepted for publication the author begins to work with an editor in the same way you might work with a teacher on your book. The first step between the editor and author/illustrator is a legal contract, or written agreement. If the author is working through a literary agent, the agent takes care of this step. Each contract is different, but all contain basic terms stating which duties are the author's or illustrator's (submitting the material by a certain date, preparing it in a certain manner, etc.) and which duties are the publisher's (producing the book by a certain date, promoting, advertising, and making it available to the buyer, etc.). The contract also specifies the *royalty rate*, which is the percentage of the selling price to be paid to the author and/or illustrator. *Note*: An author never pays to have his book published by a reputable company; he is always paid by them on terms mutually agreed on at the time of preparing the contract.

The author and the editor then begin work on the book. The editor makes suggestions about content, style, and organization of the material. The editor may request the author to rework or rewrite certain parts of the manuscript. To visualize the manuscript in terms of a finished book, the editor works with specialists on the publisher's staff to determine size, format, and type of artwork or photographs, if any. The editor may suggest an illustrator to the author or, as with this book, the author may be the illustrator as well. Some books have only pictures, with no words, and then the editor and illustrator work together without an author. The specialists with whom the editor consults at this stage are members of the *production department*, the *art department*, and the *sales department*. These people all work together to produce an attractive book that will sell for a reasonable price to stores, schools, and libraries.

After the author completes the mauscript, it must be checked by a skilled *copy editor*, who examines details of literary style, organization, and fact, as well as correcting mistakes in spelling, grammar, and punctuation.

The corrected manuscript is then worked on by the production department. The *designer* plans the details of typography, such as which type faces will be used and in what sizes, how many words there should be on each line and how many lines on each page, how wide the margins will be. Then the manuscript is marked with directions for the person who will set it in type (the compositor). The designer also selects the color, size, and type of paper for pages and dust jacket, material for binding, size of illustrations, and supervises the technique used to prepare the art. Here the designer and illustrator must work closely with the *production manager* who must decide which type of printing press will give the best results at reasonable cost.

When a book has many illustrations which must be arranged around areas of text, a *dummy* like the one you made in Chapter III, Section B, is made either by the art department or by the illustrator. The dummy indicates the layout, or arrangement by pages, of the text and illustrations. It is used by the designer, and sometimes the printer, to make sure everything gets into its proper place.

D. What Does the Printer Do?

The manuscript is sent to the printer (*compositor*), where it is set in type according to the notes written by the designer and the corrections and styling notes made by the copy editor. When the compositor is finished, copies of what he has set in type (called *galley proofs*) are made and sent to the publisher who sends a set to the author, and sometimes the illustrator. Another set is sent to the editor and copy editor. The galleys are read carefully for mistakes—which may be the printer's *typographical errors* (upside down, or inverted, letters or words, transposed lines, etc.) or misspellings or errors in grammar not previously caught by the author or copy editor. Corrections to be made in the galleys are indicated with *proofreader's marks*, special

have you ever wanted to make your own book—to illustrate and bind a story you wrote yourself? Anyone of any can enjoy the craft of bookmaking, explained here in smiple, step-by-step illustrated instructions, using every day materials.

symbols which you can find listed in a dictionary. You see illustrated a proof corrected with these marks. Although a great many people work hard to correct mistakes in proofs, a few manage to slip through every now and then. If you find a mistake in a book, you can write to the publisher to tell him. If possible, it will be corrected when the book is reprinted.

Galleys marked for correction are returned to the printer, who corrects the errors and makes a second set of proofs in which the lines of type are divided so the correct number will fit onto each page. These are called *page proofs*, and once again they must be checked for errors. Now that the page numbers are known, an index may be made.

A compositor correcting galley proofs on an Intertype machine.

One type of galley proving press.

The next, and last, proofs are called *reproduction proofs* (repros) and are carefully printed on special paper so the type will be sharp, clear, and reproduce well.

While the compositor has been working to prepare the text for reproduction, the illustrator and designer have been working to prepare the art. The art, too, must be changed into a form suitable for printing. The printer takes the art, neatly labeled for proper placement in the book, and photographs it, as explained in Section F of this chapter. The negatives of the art and the text are then stripped together and converted into printing plates. Plates are made of metal, plastic, or molded rubber depending on the type of press and printing method used.

E. How Are Books Printed?

Today most books are printed on offset presses, though some books are still printed by the letterpress method. Both methods usually require large presses, some the size of one or two school buses put together. Both use paper in large sheets or rolls. If rolled paper is used, it unwinds while running through the press and is then cut into sheets by a large cutting blade. At the bindery each sheet is folded into a *signature* by a method similar to that described in Chapter VIII,

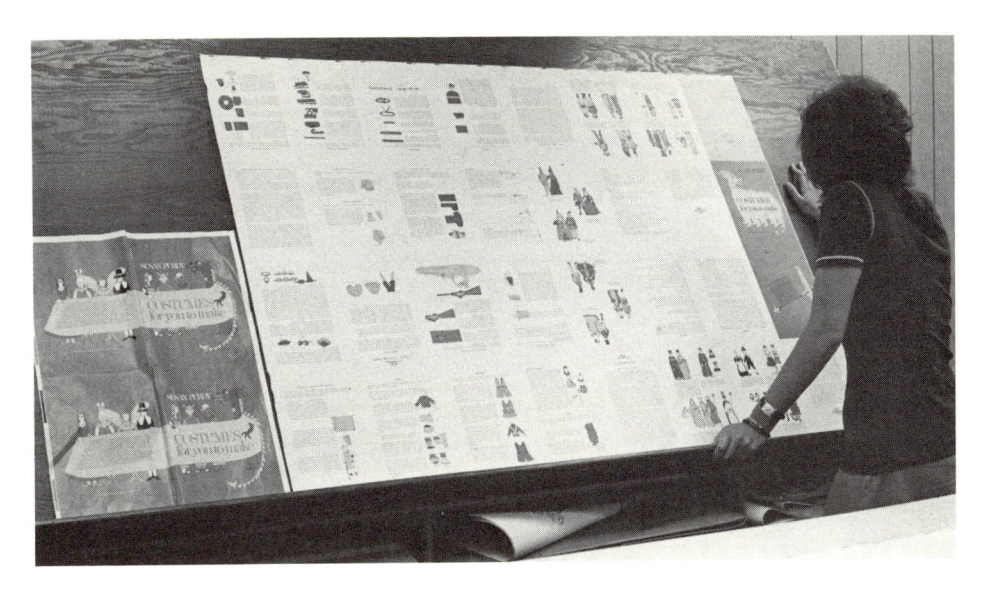

Checking a large press sheet, which contains the images of 32 pages on each side. Cover proofs are at left.

Section B. A sheet may be run through the press several times—once to print each side in black ink and once for each additional color ink to be used. There are some very large presses that can print several colors in one operation.

Letterpress printing is not as common as it once was in the book industry because modern offset presses are faster and have greater flexibility in reproducing artwork. You will be more familiar with the letterpress method, however, because it is similar to that of a small hand printing press or a block print. The set type is locked together in a metal frame called a *chase*. A small number of copies may be printed simply by inking a chase directly and pressing paper down on it. However, in this way, the metal will wear down after long use. To protect it, plates are made by first making molds from the chase, then pouring a thin layer of liquid metal, plastic, or rubber onto the molds. When the metal hardens and is turned out, it forms the printing plate, a reproduction of the chase.

Although set metal type is used to make the text plates, the artwork must first be *photoengraved*. Pieces of artwork are held up on a vertical plane and photographed by a special large camera. The negative is then placed on top of a metal plate covered with a light-sensitive

Letterpress type locked into a chase.

chemical. The negative is held firmly in place, exposed to light for a short time, then removed. The plate is then washed with developing chemicals which remove the blank areas of the page and leave slightly raised areas to be printed. Plates containing both text and art are set in the press, inked with a wide cylinder called a *roller*, and then the paper is pressed against the inked plate picking up the image.

In *offset* printing the type and the artwork are photographed together. The photonegatives for many pages at once are arranged and taped together on a large sheet of special paper. This *flat* of negatives is turned into an *offset plate* by photoetching, a process whereby the image is transferred to the light-sensitive surface of a large thin zinc or aluminum plate by using chemicals. In its simplest form, the basic offset press uses five cylinders, or rollers. The etched plate is fastened to one cylinder which is then washed with water by a second cylinder. Then the plate is inked by a third cylinder passing over it. The first cylinder then transfers or "offsets" the inked image onto a fourth, rubber-coated cylinder, which prints the image onto the fifth, paper-covered cylinder.

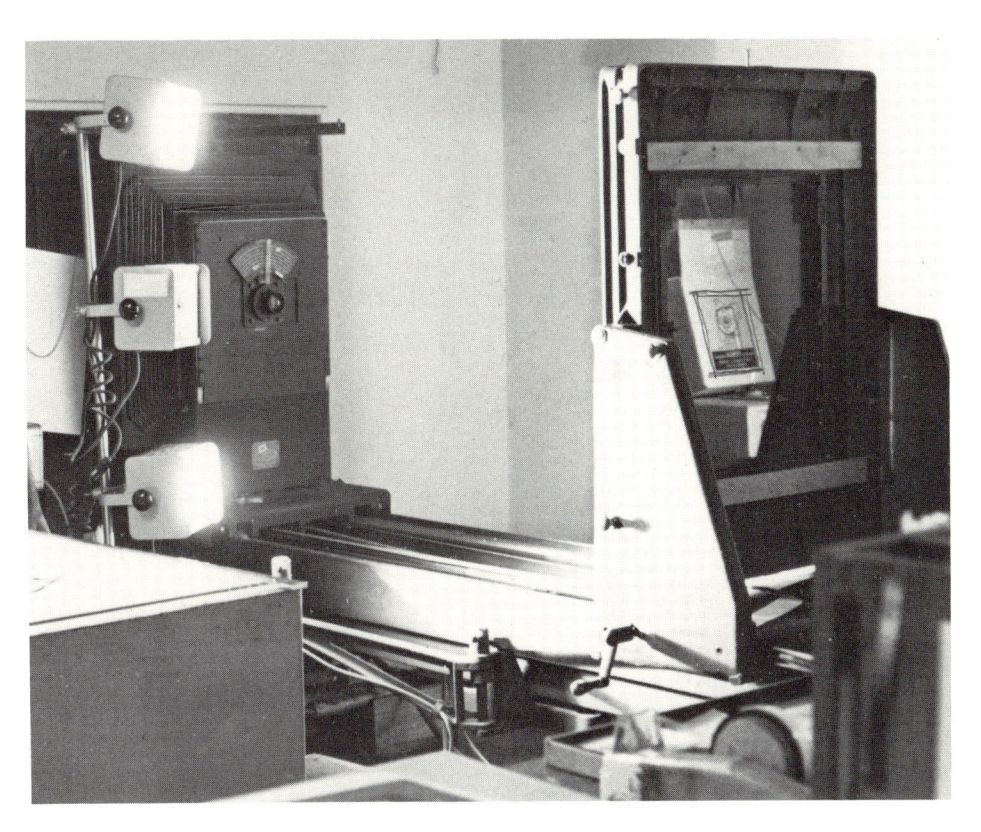

Artwork (on right panel) being photographed by special camera.

Arranging and taping negatives on light table.

Wiping a photoetched plate with developing chemicals.

Putting ink into trough on an offset press.

Offset press. Unprinted sheets stacked in foreground.

Suction hoses lifting printed sheets off the press.

F. How Is Artwork Printed?

Different types of artwork require different types of preparation for printing. Some of the preparation is done by the printer, some of it is done by the artist. Black and white line drawings with flat areas of black can be printed in the same way as type. It is photographed and the negative is used to make the printing plate. This is called *line art*. Line art can also be printed in color by using colored ink.

Artwork with shaded tones of gray or shaded color (such as a watercolor painting) is called *halftone art*. This cannot be reproduced as it is; the printer changes it into line art by a technique that transforms the shaded tones into groups of dots to create an optical illusion: the eye is tricked into blending the dots with the paper color to make tones which are not truly there. The art is turned into dots by being photographed through a *screen* made of a mesh of crossed lines. The number of lines on a screen depends on the smoothness of the paper to be printed on. On finely reproduced illustrations, the dots are so tiny you can hardly see them. Rough paper (such as newsprint) requires bigger mesh to make larger dots that will show up on the irregular surface. Look carefully at a comic book or newspaper picture —with or without a magnifying glass—and you will see the dots.

LINE ART

HALFTONE ART

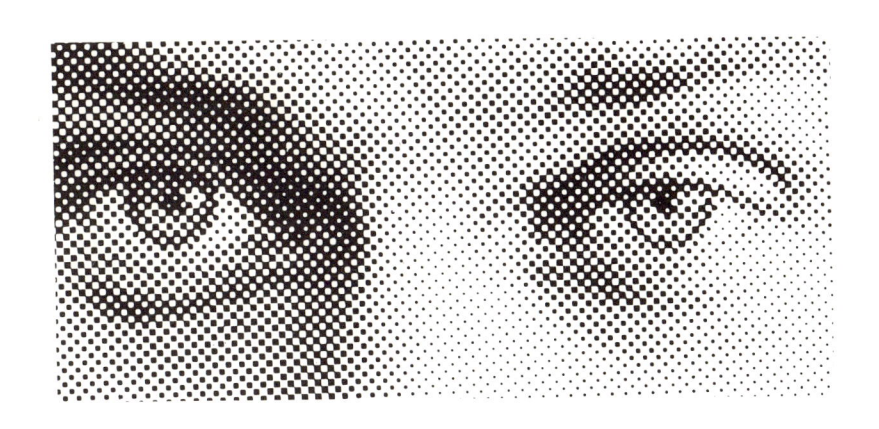

HALFTONE ART PHOTOGRAPHED THROUGH SCREEN MAKING DOT PATTERN

(SQUINT TO SEE IMAGE CLEARLY)

If the artwork is to be printed in color, the colors must be separated from each other so they can be printed one at a time. If it has colors blending into one another to make still other colors, like the lion painting shown here, the only way to separate the colors is by camera. Printers use cameras with special filters that screen out the primary colors (red, yellow, and blue) in turn. For example, a green filter allows only red to pass through, making the red plate. A photograph is taken and made into a plate for each color: red, yellow, and blue, and black. On the printing press, the plates are printed in sequence to allow the inks to mix with each other properly. When each separate color plate is printed over the other, the layers combine to make the finished print.

Sometimes the artwork is preseparated by the artist, instead of the camera. In *preseparated* artwork, the artist makes a key drawing (a), with *register marks* set down in the margins. A series of overlays, one for each color (b, c, d), is made on sheets of transparent paper or acetate; each overlay is fastened over the key drawing, labeled, and marked with register marks that line up exactly with the marks on the drawing below. Overlays are photographed separately by the printer and turned into plates in the same manner as line art. When the plates are inked with color and printed over each other, you can see the complete image (e). The importance of careful registering can be seen in comic books, newspapers, or magazines where you often see pictures "out of register," the red of a mouth, for example, fallen slightly from its proper position.

**Preseparated artwork
prepared by artist**

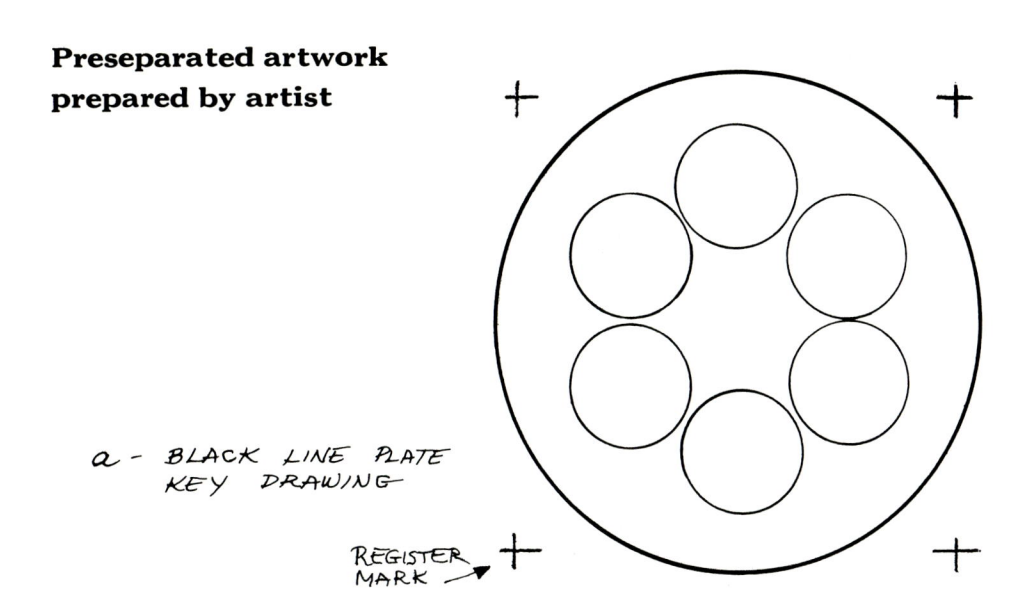

a - BLACK LINE PLATE
    KEY DRAWING

REGISTER MARK →

NOTE: OVERLAYS ARE ORIGINALLY PAINTED IN BLACK.
       PROOFS OF COLORED INKS ARE SHOWN TO
       ONE SIDE.

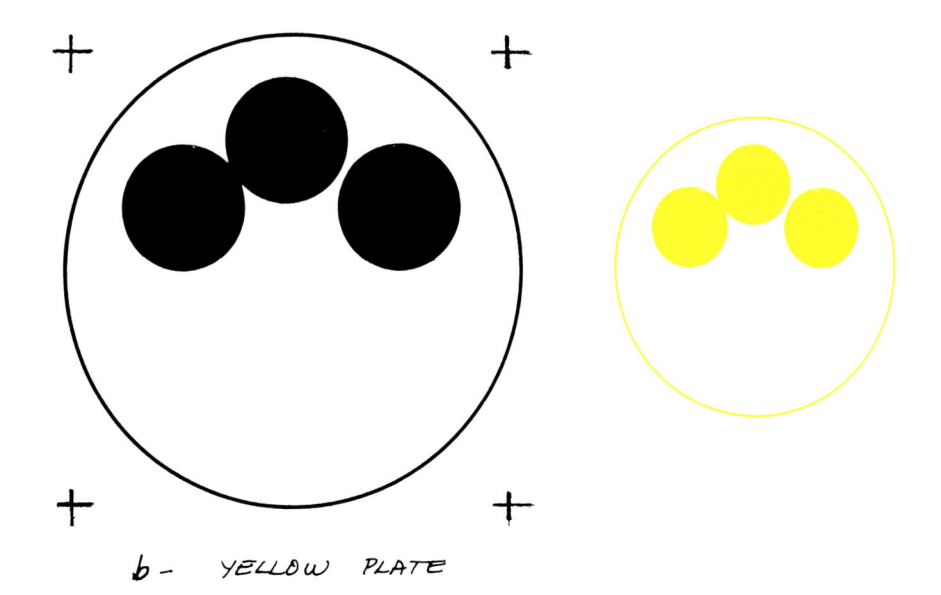

b - YELLOW PLATE

c - RED PLATE

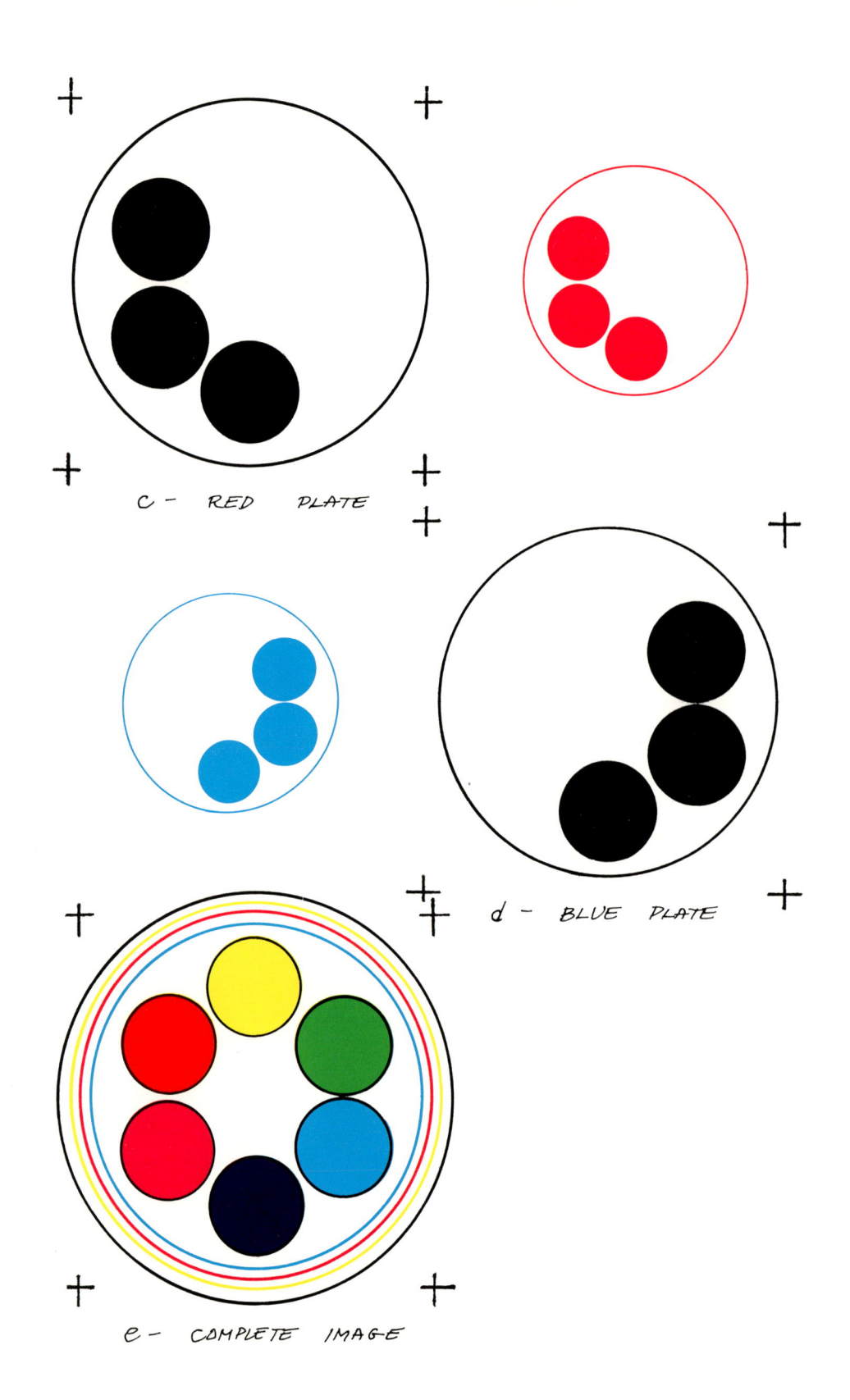

d - BLUE PLATE

e - COMPLETE IMAGE

Color art separated by camera

Black Plate

Yellow Plate

Red Plate

Blue Plate

Full Color Print

G. How Are Printed Sheets Turned Into Bound Books?

After the sheets are printed, they are sent to the *bindery*. At the bindery, a special *folding and gathering machine* with many "arms" fold up each sheet in a specific order making a signature. (See Chapter

The gathering machine has many arms which pick up the signatures in correct order.

VIII, Section B). The endpapers are then added and a large sewing machine is used to stitch the signatures together in a manner similar to the one you used in Chapter VIII, Section B. Still another machine

A signature is placed in the sewing machine, spools of thread at top.

flattens the signatures by "smashing" out the air from between the pages. It then trims the pages evenly, rounds the spine, and reinforces it with glue and, often, with a strip of mull as in Chapter VIII, Section D. Some binding machines are big enough and complex enough to do all these steps in a single operation.

Stacks of sewn signatures going through smashing machine. Smaller stack in back is already smashed.

Still another machine prepares the case as you did in Chapter VIII, Section D, by covering the front, back, and spine boards with cloth or

Pressing three pieces of cover board onto covering material to make case.

paper. Finally the book is fastened to the covers, or "cased-in," and the endpapers are glued down. Last, the finished books are inspected for defects (tears, ill-made bindings, etc.), wrapped in dust jackets, packed, and shipped to the publisher's warehouse. From there they go to stores, schools, and libraries that have placed orders for them. If a book is popular and all the copies printed are sold, it will be reprinted. If it does not sell well, it will eventually be declared "out of print" by the publisher and will no longer be available.

Casing-in of a book. Completed book comes off machine at top of picture.

H. How Long Does It Take to Make a Book?

As you know after having read this chapter, the writing, illustrating, editing, printing, and binding of a book involve a lot of people, machines, and time. An author and/or illustrator may have been thinking about the idea for the book for months or years, and actually working on it for anywhere from a few months to a few years before completion. Publishers generally allow from six to twelve months between the time they receive the complete manuscript and artwork and the time they expect to have bound books ready for sale. The long-awaited date on which a book is ready for you to read is called the *publication date*, and is the book's official birthday. Publishers sometimes give a publication party for a new book and its author; perhaps you will want to have a party to celebrate the "birthday" of your very own handmade book.

INDEX

Appendix, 74
Art department, of publishing house, 77
Artist. See Illustrator
Artwork, 17, 80, 83, 86-88. See also Illustrations
Author, 12, 13, 76, 77

Back matter, 17, 72, 74
Bamboo strips, 11
Beeswax, 27
Bibliography, 75
Bindery, 80, 89
Binding: basic styles of, 14, 22; brass fastener, 22, 34-35; history of, 11; hole guides for sewn, 28; materials, 24; mull, 60; multi-signature, full-bound with case, 23, 57; perfect, 72; repairing, 23; selection of, 19, 22; sewn, 22, 35; simple, 32; single sheets sewn to hinged boards, 22, 36; single-signature, sewn, 23, 45; stapled, 22, 32-33; tapes, 60; vocabulary, 14
Birthday, of book, 93
Bleed, 16, 21
Blurb, 68
Boards, 36, 48, 53, 62, 71, 91. See also Cardboard
Bookbinding. See Binding
Books: birthday of, 93; contents of printed, 72; designing, 15, 17; editing, 77-78; history of, 11; illustrating, 19-20; making of, 76; parts of bound, 14; printing, 76-92; publishing, 76, 93; writing, 12-13. See also Binding

Cardboard, 25, 26
Case, 14, 57, 61, 91
Casing-in, 92

Chase, letterpress, 81-82
Chinese: ancient books made by, 11; language, writing of, 73
Cloth. See Fabric
Codex, 11
Color, 17, 18-20, 88. See also Illustrations
Compositor, 79. See also Printer
Contract, 77
Copy editor, 78
Copyright, 73
Corners, covered, 52
Corrections. See Revisions
Cover, 11, 14, 21, 63. See also Boards; Dust Jacket
Cutting, 26, 27

Dedication, 74
Designer, 15, 74, 78
Design, of book, 15-21. See also Illustrations
Double-page spread, 73
Dummy, 13, 14, 16, 21, 78
Dust jacket, 14, 68-69, 75, 92

Editor, 73, 77
Egyptian writing, 11
Endpapers, 14, 16, 17, 21, 42, 92
Epigraph, 74

Fabric, 21, 25, 26
Fiction, 12
Fixing, of artwork, 21
Flap copy, 68
Flyleaf, 14
Folding, 27, 89
Folios, 14, 19
Foot, 14
Fore-edge, 14
Foreword, 74
Front matter, 17, 72
Full-bound, 14, 57

Galley proofs, 78-80
Gathering, 89

Glossary, 74
Glue, 24
Grain, 26, 27
Greeks, scrolls of ancient, 11
Gutenberg, Johann, 12

Half-bound, 14, 48
Half-title, 73
Halftone art, 86, 87
Head, 14
Hebrew language, writing of, 73
Hinge and hinge strip, 36, 38
Hole-measuring guides, 28-29
Holland, movable type in, 11

Ideas, for writing, 12, 77
Illustrations: planning and placement of, 15, 16, 19, 21; printing of, 86-88; techniques for, 20
Illustrator, 19, 73, 77, 78, 88
Index, 75
Initials, decorative, 18
Inks, 11, 82, 84, 88
Introduction, 74

Japanese language, writing of, 73

Layout, 15-17
Letterpress, 81, 82
Library of Congress, 74
Line art, 86
Linotype, 79
Literary agent, 76

Mailing of manuscripts, 76
Manuscript, 12, 13, 17, 18, 76
Margins, 16, 17, 18
Materials, 24
Mediums, for artwork, 21
Mending books, 23

94

Middle Ages, 11
Mull, 60, 90

Nonfiction, 12
Numbering. *See* Folios

Oddments, 72
Offset, 80, 82, 85
Oriental books, 73
Overlays, 88

Paper: art, 20-21; book page, 16, 18, 20, 25; case cover, 63; -covered board, 53; cutting of, 26; dummy layout, 17; dust jacket, 69; folding of, 27; for printing press, 80; history of, 11; reproduction proof, 80
Paperbacks, 72
Papyrus, 11
Parchment, 11
Pens, 11, 18
Photoengraving, 81
Photoetching, 82, 84
Photographs, 21, 80, 83
Pictures. *See* Illustrations
Plates, printing, 80-82
Poetry, 12
Preface, 74
Preseparated artwork, 88
Presses, printing, 80-82, 84-85

Printer, 78, 80
Printing, 21, 72, 76, 81, 86
Production manager, 78
Production process, 77-78
Proofs, 78-81
Proofreader's marks, 78
Prose, 12
Publication date, 93
Publisher, 73, 76, 77

Quarter-bound, 14

Readers, of manuscripts, 76
Rebinding. *See* Repairing books
Register, 88
Repairing books, 23
Revisions, of manuscript, 13, 76
Rollers, 82
Royalties, 77

Sales department, of publishing house, 77
Scribe, 11
Scrolls, 11
Separations, of color, 88
Sewing, 25, 28, 30-31, 90
Sheets, printed, 80, 81, 85, 89. See Signature(s)
Signature(s), 14, 45; folding and sewing a single, 45, 80; full-bound with case, 57; gathering of, 89; sewing machine for, 90; sewn, 58; single, half-bound, 48
Skills, basic, 26
Smashing, 90, 91
Spine, 14, 40, 49, 62
Straight edge, cutting of, 26
Stylus, 11
Supplies. *See* Materials

Tape recorder, 12, 76
Tapes, binding, 60
Text, 18-20, 80-81. *See also* Manuscript
Thread, 25, 27
Title page, 73
Translator, 73
Type, 11, 12, 15, 18, 78, 82
Type faces, 18. *See also* Type
Typewriter, 12, 76
Typographer, 74
Typographical errors, 78
Typography. *See* Type

Unsolicited manuscripts, 77

Writer, 11. *See also* Author
Writing, 12, 13, 18

About the Author

Susan Purdy was born in New York City and grew up in Connecticut. Educated at Vassar College and New York University, she spent her junior year at the Sorbonne and the Ecôle des Beaux Arts in Paris. Mrs. Purdy was a textile designer in New York City until her marriage; she and her husband now live in Connecticut in a house they designed and built themselves. Mrs. Purdy writes and illustrates children's books, and designs various craft projects which appear in national women's magazines. Until recently, she taught children's private art classes and codirected and taught art at a music-and-art day camp. An essential part of the camp art program was creative experimentation with materials and design, and she has drawn on this experience in adapting many creative art techniques to the material in her popular activities and craft books. For several years, Mrs. Purdy has lectured and demonstrated the art of book-making at libraries and schools from the elementary to the college level. Her workshops, in which young people write, illustrate, and bind their own books, showed the need, and provided the inspiration, for this book.